I0953792

Bernard Meltzer Solves Your Money Problems

Borrowing, buying, and investment strategies to profit from inflation

by Bernard Meltzer

SIMON AND SCHUSTER

NEW YORK

SIMON AND SCHUSTER and colophon are trademarks of Simon & Schuster
Designed by Irving Perkins Associates

Manufactured in the United States of America

I wish to thank Harold Prince, my very good friend, without whose encouragement and help this book never could have been written.

*To my beloved and beautiful wife, Phyllis,
to the millions of members of my radio family
who are responsible for my success, and to
all the wonderful people who have helped me
become "a human being"*

Contents

Introduction:

Hi-yuh! This Is Your Friend Bernard Meltzer

I WANT TO TALK TO YOU

Over the last fifteen years, tens of thousands of people have called in to my radio shows and said, in essence, "Dr. Meltzer, I have a problem. I need help." I pride myself that in a few minutes the anxiety is gone from each caller's voice, and a happy person is saying, "Thank you."

I solve problems by talking. I wish I could solve your problems by talking to you. But although in the future you may be able to open an electronic book and have a conversation with the author, right now I can't talk to you from these pages. So what I've done is the next best thing—I've written this book in the same way as I talk.

I speak your language—simple, direct, using words we both understand. I don't use language to show how smart I am and to belittle my audience. I use language the way it was meant to be used—to get over facts and ideas, no matter how complex, as easily and as rapidly as possible. One of my idols, one of the greatest men in history, was Winston Churchill, the brilliant British statesman who rallied his nation to defeat the vicious attacks of Adolf Hitler. Churchill's ideas are profound, but as you read his books there's not an idea of his that you can't grasp at once. That's because his language was basic—it was the language of the people. So is mine, for a different time and a different people. With my basic language I can explain the most complicated financial matters so that you can put them to use in your life at once. That's the real test of any communication whose purpose is to help.

To my scholarly and professional friends—and particularly to the writers of money books who assume every reader has a Ph.D. in economics, and who fill their pages with statistics and graphs—I wish to say: This book is not for you. This book is also not for the rich who want to get richer, for the speculator who wants to make a killing, for the lazy who want something for nothing, or for the shady characters who spend their lives in search of loopholes to riches. Let me tell you whom I'm talking to in these pages:

I'm talking to the average American. You can be starting out in life, a young woman or a young man looking ahead to prosperity and happiness. You can be a mother or father, going through all the trials and tribulations of raising a family. You can be a retiree, trying to reap the rewards of a long life of usefulness and devotion. You can be anybody in any walk of life who is faced with the serious money problems of the '80s, all of which center around the problem of inflation.

I'm particularly qualified to answer your money problems, for two reasons. One reason is that I wear many hats. Some people know me as an engineer; others as a college professor, a real estate expert, an educator, a builder, a city planner, an expert in property evaluation, an investment analyst, an authority in urban problems, a successful businessman, or an expert legal witness. The second reason is that as a financial expert on WOR radio in New York and WCAU radio in Philadelphia I have over the last fifteen years answered more than 100,000 questions asked me on the air and more than 300,000 questions sent to me in the mail. The questions come from members of my audience—my radio family—who are very much like you.

WHAT THIS BOOK CAN DO FOR YOU

In this book I'm going to talk to you about how you can actually profit from inflation. The basic strategy—the general plan—is both to buy and to invest with borrowed dollars. The reason for that is, because of inflation you pay back your loan with dollars that shrink in value from month to month, from year to year. In actuality, inflation makes it possible to pay back a dollar with a dollar worth 90¢, then 80¢, then 70¢, and so on. I'm also going to talk to you about credit strategies that can go to work for you when you buy virtually anything, and when you put borrowed money (as well as your own) in safe investments that are certain to bring in returns higher than the rate of inflation.

After my introductory section, this book is composed of three sections. They are:

Solving Your Borrowing Problems: How to Get the Money You Need When You Need It, where you'll find everything you ever wanted to know about borrowing, including how to get your loan requests approved.

Solving Your Buying Problems: How to Buy Your Home, Your Car, and Almost Anything You Need on Credit, which contains detailed information on the two most important and costly purchases you're likely to make, your home and your car; plus guidelines on how to turn your credit card into one of the most valuable financial tools ever invented. And—

Solving Your Investment Problems: How to Make the Safest, Most Profitable Investments—Using Borrowed Money (and Your Own), from which you'll obtain prudent advice on inflation-beating investments from CDs to gold.

I don't know of any other book which links together all the aspects of your financial life—borrowing, buying, and investing—with a strategy for profiting from inflation. That strategy is the basic answer to all your money problems.

HOW TO USE THIS BOOK

I've worked hard to make this book very, very simple to use. I've modeled the format after the one devised by Dr. Spock. A long time ago when I was a young father, I used Dr. Spock's world-famous book on child care as my guide, for the simple reason that I could extract specific information from it with no trouble at all. For example, when I wanted to know why my two-year-old was coughing at two o'clock in the morning, I turned to the section dealing with two-year-olds and looked for the subsection *Coughing*.

You can do the same kind of thing with this book. For example, when you want to know the kind of options that are right for you when you buy a car, look in the detailed table of contents for the part which deals with How to Buy, which is Part II, then look for the chapter on Buying Your Car, which is Chapter 8, and finally find the section *How to decide about options*, which is Section 37. The sections contain all the hard-core information you want. Each section head is preceded by a numeral for quick identification. It would be a good idea if you studied the table of contents for a few minutes to get a bird's-eye view of the wealth of material in this book which can be of help in solving your money problems.

When there seem to be pros and cons about the best way to solve a problem, I'll tell you what I think is best. Look for my decisions in boxes with headings that begin BERNARD MELTZER'S ADVICE. The best thing about these boxes is that you can get the answer you're looking for in seconds. These boxed capsules of advice are listed in the table of contents. Also, as you read through the book you'll find I'm not shy about expressing my opinions about money and related matters. For quick reading, I've summed up some of these opinions under the heading *Meltzerism*. I've also included stories about real people with problems like yours (but I haven't used real names).

And one further aid: The *details*—not the principles—of everything I talk about in this book change from day to day. Nobody's ever lived in a time of history when the monetary facts of daily life were changing so fast. So at the end of this book, I've added a list of places where you can write for information, in almost all cases without charge. It will help you put the principles in this book to instant use.

I believe you will use this book in your daily life with profit. But who, you might very well ask, is this man who can make such a statement? Who is this man whose advice you're going to rely on? In all fairness to yourself, before you start listening to my advice, you should know more about me. So—

LET ME INTRODUCE MYSELF

*"Hi-*yuh! This is your friend Bernard Meltzer." If you're a member of my radio family, you'll recognize the greeting. This is the way I open my radio show *What's Your Problem?* which beams from WOR in New York. More than a million people listen to it every hour in the metropolitan area, and several millions more listen to it outside. My show, which deals mostly with money problems, but actually covers everything from finance to romance, has the largest audience of any radio station in any time slot in the nation. I seldom receive less than 5,000 letters and calls a week from people of all ages in all walks of life from some thirty states and six Canadian provinces. *The Wall Street Journal* reported, "Mr. Meltzer has won unflagging devotion from his listeners." *The New Yorker* magazine wrote, "Meltzer is not simply popular; he is adored."

Why do I have such a large and devoted following? I'll point up the basic reason with the story of how I broke into radio in the first place. It's 1966, and a famous radio personality has his own show on WCAU Philadelphia on Saturday mornings from ten to twelve. This Friday night he comes into the studio and says to the station manager, "Sorry about this, but I've got a new job in Washington, gotta pack tomorrow morning, and I can't handle the show." The station manager is all upset, he gets on the phone, calls a lot of professionals, but it's Friday night, and sometimes nobody's home, and sometimes they say, "I can't get ready by tomorrow morning," and the upshot is he comes up with nobody.

He's frantic, and he calls me. He calls me because at this time I had a newspaper column in the *Philadelphia Bulletin,* I was a professor at Pennsylvania University, I had been lecturing for years, and I had been a guest on the station a week before. So he remembers me. He says to me, "Take over the show this Saturday, and the next Saturday. I'll give you $50 for each show." For a radio station to pay *anything* without a contract, that was astonishing. I was flattered, and I said I'd be in, and he said, "Come in early—I want you to watch a real pro at work, so you can pick up some pointers."

I come in, and I sit down in the studio, and this "real pro" was running a call-in show, the kind of show I've been doing ever since, and he says to me, "Look, the phones are not lighting up"—which means nobody's calling in—and he says, "Let me show you a trick of the trade, which you'll use as long as you're on the air. I'm gonna get those phones to light up." At this time, there's a woman calling in, and she's rambling and not making too much sense. He says to her, "Madam, how old are you?" She says, "Seventy-two." He says, "Madam, if you've reached seventy-two, and you don't have more sense than you have, you shouldn't be calling up anybody," and he hangs up. Almost immediately, all his phones—there must have been eight or ten of them —they all light up. He had used that old lady to stir up a lot of protest calls. It may have been a trick of the trade, but I think it's a dirty trick, and I say to myself, "I'm not going to use it, I'm not going to imitate anything he does. I'm just going to be myself, and I'll see what happens."

I go on at ten, and I have no trouble lighting up the phones. When the show's over, I walk over to the station manager's office, and I say to him, "How'd I do?" He says to me, "I've been in this business for a long time, and your program was the worst I've ever heard in my life." I say to him, "Why do you say that?" He says, "Do you really want me to tell you?" I say, "Yes." He says, "You don't have the voice of a professional. On radio you must have a cultured voice, a booming voice. You have the voice of an ordinary man in the street. You mispronounce words. Don't you know when you do that, people turn you off? And worst of all, you butchered the commercials." Then he says to me,

"Don't feel badly. What you do in life, you do very well. You're just not cut out for radio."

My ego is bruised, and I slink away feeling I'll never be on radio again. The next Friday, the station manager calls. "Bernie," he says, "you're coming in tomorrow?" "No," I say, "my ego trip is over," and I hang up. He calls again. "Listen, Bernie, I'm just asking you a simple question: Are you coming in tomorrow?" I think he's taunting me, and I say, "Stop torturing me," and I hang up again. He calls up again and he says, "Listen, I'm coming down to see you," and *he* hangs up. He comes down, and he says, "Bernie, I want to admit I'm embarrassed. You know how many letters that time spot used to pull? One, maybe two. You know how many letters you pulled? Two-three hundred! And what's more, sponsors are calling in. They want to be on your show! They actually like the honest way you did the commercials. Bernie, I don't know what it is you've got, but you're a success."

I know what I've "got." The secret of my success on radio then, and ever since, is—being myself. And what's "myself"? What kind of man am I? What makes me tick? You have the right to know. Here I am going to help you solve your money problems—solve them sometimes in ways experts will tell you are "crazy"—and you don't know a thing about me. You should know all about me if you're going to have faith in my advice, because what I am determines what kind of advice I give.

I am the sum of all the influences on me from the day I was born. I was molded by my parents, by where I was brought up, by how I was brought up, by the kids I grew up with, by where I went to school and college, by war, and by the important people in my life. You can only understand the kind of man I am by understanding those influences and their effects on me. So come back with me to when it all started, to a glorious time when emigrant families like mine came to these shores believing that the streets of America were paved with gold.

1.

I was born into a family, a neighborhood, a small wonderful section of the world, where everybody believed America is, and always has been, and always will be, the shining land of opportunity, the only place in the world where dreams come true. To this day when I read my Bible and come across God's promise of a land of milk and honey, I know that promise has been fulfilled. That land of milk and honey is right here. It's our America. But what's so strange is that this belief could be so strong in my family and in my neighborhood, because in those days all of us were living in grinding poverty.

I was born on the Lower East Side of Manhattan in the shadow of the Williamsburg Bridge. We lived in a tenement on the corner of Attorney and Broome streets. We were one block away from Delancey Street, the Broadway of the Lower East Side. It was a wide street with all sorts of shops and restaurants; and the excitement and bustle of people on it, the feeling of great forces of life erupting on it, is one of the most treasured of the memories of my boyhood. Delancey Street was a place of ferment, of vigor, of promises of things to come—a symbol of the whole Jewish ghetto that clustered around it. But while spirits were high in the ghetto back there in the early '20s, the standard of living was low.

We lived in a five-story walkup. On each floor there were four apartments—two in the front and two in the back. Between front and back was a toilet—not a bathroom, a toilet—which was used by all four families on the floor. There was not only no bathroom, there was no hot water. So we could have baths, my mother would bring a big washtub into the kitchen and heat up water on the coal-fired stove. Later, when my father began to earn more money, we graduated to a gas stove—but not like today's gas stove. The gas was regulated by a coin-operated meter. My mother put a quarter in the meter for a certain amount of gas; then when we used that amount, the gas shut off automatically. Sometimes we would get ready for our bath—and in the winter it got pretty cold—and the meter would shut off while the water was still only lukewarm, and my mother would go racing around the house searching or another quarter while we all shivered. It was too expensive to heat up separate tubs for each of the kids—there were four of us, two boys and two girls—so we each took turns using the same water, the oldest first, then the next oldest, and so on. I was number three.

Before we had gas, my job was to bring up the coal. Families who were pretty well off could stock up with a ton of coal which they stored in bins in the basement (each family had its own bin). But we never had the money, so once a week my mother would call, "Beryl"—that's my name in Yiddish—"we're running out of coal," and I'd walk down about three blocks, then lug a fifty-pound sack back with me. I was a husky kid, and I was glad—actually, proud—to help. One of the things that I learned in those days is that a family has to help each other, and if one is stronger than the others—and I don't mean just physically; you can be stronger in character or in brains or in leadership—then the one that's stronger should do the most helping. A family can only be happy and prosper if everybody does his share according to his abilities. And helping each other, taking on responsibilities, makes for happiness all around. We were a happy family.

The conditions under which we lived never got us down—and looking back, those conditions were pretty rough. In the summer the place was like a furnace; in the winter the only heated room in the flat was the kitchen, and we ate, slept, worked, bathed, passed all our days and nights there, all six of us. When spring came around, we moved out of the kitchen. But there were only two other rooms in the flat, a bedroom, which was shared by my father, my mother, my younger sister, and, when I was very young, me; and a living room, in which my older sister slept on a couch. My older brother slept in the kitchen all year around.

Overcrowding, no heat, no hot running water, no bathroom, one toilet for four families—why, if any family had to live like that today, what a howl of protest would go up from the do-gooders. These days the government puts up some housing projects for the underprivileged with air conditioning, swimming pools, and recreation halls. If people had to live today the way we lived in the '20s, social workers would write articles and go on television predicting that the kids would grow up antisocial and become criminals, and that bad housing was the root of all evil. But the curious thing was, we didn't feel deprived; so how could we become antisocial? We knew we weren't rich, but we never felt poor. As young kids we didn't even realize we were living in a slum. And as we grew older and learned that other people lived better than we did, we weren't envious, we weren't resentful. We felt that our status was temporary, something we all had to pass through before we could go on to higher things. We had hope. We knew that in America anybody could make anything he wanted to make of himself. Our childhood in the ghetto was a time of dreaming dreams, golden dreams, that we would make come true as time passed by.

I had a shining example in my own family of making a dream come true. My father had come to New York in 1906 from a small village in Poland, so poor that he had to leave my mother and older sister and brother behind. His first big dream was to earn enough money to bring his loved ones over here. He couldn't speak the language, he had no education outside of Hebrew school—and that was very little use in America—but he had faith and courage, and he worked hard. Oh, did he work hard. From early morning until late at night, he drove around town in a horse and wagon peddling seltzer water. It came in bottles with spigots on them, and it was regarded as a great treat in Jewish households. But the profits were small, and it took my father ten years of working every day of the week except the sabbath to get enough money together to send for his family. Ten years of hard work, but one dream had come true, everybody was together. Then on to another dream: peddler no more, a businessman instead. He saved up his money and became a sort of entrepreneur, moving from one kind of business to another, but always moving ahead. And then he made another dream come true: We moved out of the ghetto. I was eleven years old when we went to live in Williamsburg.

Williamsburg is in Brooklyn, on the other side of the Williamsburg Bridge from Manhattan—only about a mile from where we had lived on the Lower East Side. But it was a far greater distance than a mile we had moved; we had moved from poverty to the middle class. The housing in Williamsburg was a mixture of apartment houses which had been built just prior to and just after World War I, and what we would now call townhouses—three- and four-story structures which had been built for a single family. But around this time—it was about 1928—many of them had been converted to three- or four-family residences with one family to a floor. My father had bought one of these townhouses. He rented out three of the floors, and we lived on the second floor. Compared to our three-room ghetto flat, this was paradise. We had hot water, we had rooms of our own, we even had our own bathroom! We were climbing.

But for me my father wanted an easier route to the top. "Beryl," he would say to me over and over again, "this is America, and you have an advantage I never had—education. You get ahead fast in America through education." New York's public schools were excellent in those days, and I had begun my education in one of them in the Lower East Side, and now I was continuing it in another in Brooklyn. But I was running into trouble. I was a victim of dyslexia.

Dyslexia is a learning disability. It's estimated that some 20 million people in this country have it in various degrees of intensity. It's manifested in childhood by the inability to read well. But it has nothing to do with IQ. You can have a very high IQ, as I had, and still have difficulty reading.

So that you can understand what I went through as a child, I'd like to show you the difference between how you read as a normal person and how I read as a dyslexiac. When you see the word "cat," you see c a t. When I saw the word "cat," I saw t a c. Just as you had to train your brain to identify c a t as "cat," so I had to train my brain to identify t a c as "cat." Now you can imagine what I was up against when the class spelled "cat" out loud c a t and I was spelling it to myself t a c.

What was right, what was wrong? I was so confused I could scarcely read anything.

In the lower grades I was thrown into a state of terror every time the teacher said, "Now we'll do reading for an hour." I tried to get around my poor reading performance in the following way. We sat in parallel rows of seats, and the teacher would say, "Row 1, Seat 1, you read a paragraph," then, "Row 1, Seat 2, you read a paragraph," and so on. I figured I would be the fifteenth kid to be called on, so I quickly counted up to the fifteenth paragraph, and I went over it and over it. By the time the teacher called on me, I was ready to just about get by. But sometimes when the teacher got to the twelfth or thirteenth kid she would say, "Johnny, that was a short paragraph. Read the next one as well," and all the work I had done on the fifteenth paragraph was wasted. I had to rush to the sixteenth paragraph, but there wasn't enough time to go over it carefully. When my turn came to read out loud, I would stutter and stumble over the words, and everybody would think I was a dope.

I felt terrible at the time, because I didn't know—and nobody else knew—that I had dyslexia. I only found that out later on. But what I did know was that something was wrong; and it was up to me to set it right. I got that habit of self-reliance from my father and from the other people in the ghetto who pulled themselves up by their own bootstraps. Patience and faith in the future is something else I learned from my father (I remembered how he had slaved for ten years to save up enough money to bring his family over from Poland); and I knew if I worked hard I could become a better reader, even if it took a long, long time. I also knew that if I became a better reader, I would become a better student and a better thinker. That was exactly what happened. While in grade school I was less than an average student, by the time I got into junior high, I was an average student, and in high school my teachers thought I was pretty close to a genius. What happened to me shows that adversity can be overcome, that you can succeed if you want to succeed. God helps those who help themselves.

In high school my brain had become so sharp that I often was able to get A's without doing the assignments. For example, we were required to read certain books, and to prove we actually read them, we had to hand in reports on the most interesting parts. What I did was open a book at random, and no matter what the page was about, that page would become the most interesting part. My brain was functioning so well that I could turn *any* page into the most interesting part without having to read the rest of the book. Teacher after teacher would say to me, "Meltzer, you picked a part nobody else ever thought of! Very perceptive! *Ve-ry* perceptive!"

Take geometry. You would think that you would have to *study* geometry—really sit down and bone up on the theorems and axioms and ways to solve problems and so forth. But I never opened my text. One day the teacher said, "Meltzer, get up there to the blackboard and bisect an angle." In the textbook, there was a detailed explanation on how to bisect an angle, but I had never seen it. I got up there, took the chalk in my hand, thought for a fraction of a minute, and then I bisected the angle. The teacher got up from his chair, went to the board, looked at my work backwards and forwards, then said in amazement, "Meltzer, do you realize you bisected an angle in a way no mathematician has ever done it before?"

The big reason I didn't do my assignments was that while I was growing up in Williamsburg I spent most of my time in the streets. As a matter of fact, I was a kind of Dead End kid. In those days there were ethnic street gangs—Italian gangs, Irish gangs, Polish gangs, German gangs—and I organized and was the leader of a Jewish gang. These gangs were nothing like the vicious street gangs that infested our cities later on. At our worst we would pilfer apples or sweet potatoes; or we'd invade another gang's territory, and some punches would be thrown—no real harm done—and that was the extent of our troublemaking. There wasn't an antisocial bone in our bodies, and we had a great respect for law and order. If fifty of my gang were strutting down the street and a cop came along and yelled, "Hey, get outta here!" we'd all run as fast as our legs would carry us. Today, it might be the cop who would run.

The gangs of my times had their own code of ethics. None of them ever touched a young lady. If an Irish gang was fighting a Jewish gang, a Jewish girl or an Irish girl could walk right through the melee and nobody would even dream of touching them. We had respect for our elders, and to assault or abuse an older person was regarded as the lowest thing you could do. What an older person said was law. Sometimes we used to snatch the covers of garbage cans to use as shields when we went to invade some other gang's territory; but if a feeble old janitor came out and yelled, "Put those garbage covers back!" we would. Stealing money was unheard of, and the idea of hitting somebody over the head and grabbing a wallet or a purse or a piece of jewelry never entered our minds. If somebody had even suggested the idea of mugging, he would have been thrown out of the gang. No adult ever felt threatened by a gang.

The gangs' basic decency resulted from the high standards of morality in the kids' homes. Our parents even frowned on the petty pilfering. I recall the time I lifted three sweet potatoes from a vegetable stand, and my mother found them in my pocket. I stole the potatoes because it was something everybody in the gang did as part of a kind of ritual. We would wait until night, build a fire in the street, roast the potatoes in it, and stand around, being together, having a good time—and even today after all those years I can still feel the burning hot sweet softness of the potatoes in my mouth, and the warmth of the fire, and the closeness of my friends. But, "It's wrong to steal," my mother shouted at me. "How could you do such a thing!" And she pulled me by the ear all the way down to the vegetable stand, where I stood with my eyes on the ground and my face red with shame while she and the vegetable man decided on my punishment. The verdict was this: two weekends working for the vegetable man without pay. And that was the end of my life of crime. Most of the boys in the gangs had similar experiences. Our parents taught us right from wrong, and we loved and respected them for it.

There was another lesson in life I learned from my parents that was even more valuable, the most valuable lesson I ever learned—that love is not just feeling, it's doing. There were times back in the ghetto days when we were so poor my mother didn't have enough food to go around. My mother would open a can of salmon—in those days that was the cheapest thing you could buy, eight or nine cents a can—and divide it up into four portions, one for each of us kids. She sat down at the table with us, but there wasn't a morsel of food on her plate; it was absolutely bare. We would ask, "Why don't you eat something, Mama?" and she would say, "I'm not hungry"; but if any of us left a scrap on the plate, she would gobble it up. She was loving by doing—doing what a devoted mother, what any devoted parent, would do: make sacrifices for the sake of the children. It's an old-fashioned virtue; and old-fashioned virtues are best.

My father's love didn't stop with the family. He loved everybody; and his deeds proved it. While we were still in the ghetto, how often did someone come knocking at our door after we were asleep, and say to my father, "Moishe Aram, so-and-so has just died," and that's all that had to be said, because whoever came knocking knew my father would take over. According to rabbinical law the dead man had to be buried the very next day. People had to be notified, but who could afford a telephone? And telegrams were only for the rich. So my father would go around and form a messenger corps—I was a member—and we'd run from tenement to tenement telling all concerned that the funeral would be tomorrow at Levine's. When the funeral was over, and my father found the widow was penniless, which was most often the case, he would go around the community, saying, "Hey, I want $10 from you . . . and I want $10 from you . . . and I want $10 from you . . ." until he had enough money to tide her over until she could get going on her own. If the man died with a little something—a passbook or an insurance policy—my father would handle all the details, and see to it that the widow got every cent that was coming to her.

Once in a while one of the kids in the neighborhood would get in trouble with the law. The mother would go almost out of her mind with grief; the old country had taught her to be terrified of the police, she couldn't speak English well, she didn't know where to go, what to do—she felt so helpless. That's when my father would step in. He would go down to the police station, get a lawyer, arrange bail. When he saw one of his friends was ill, he would run and get a doctor. In those days if you knocked at a doctor's door any time, day or night, and told him he was needed, he would take his little black satchel and go with you. As I grew up, he would send me on some of these errands of mercy—"Beryl, Beryl, run to the doctor quick—Mrs. Dobrow is very sick"—and I felt happy and proud to be helping others as he did.

But there was one aspect of life in which I couldn't help him. People came to him with their troubles. In the old country they would go to their rabbi. But in Williamsburg of the '20s and '30s, the rabbis from the old country had lost touch with reality. My father became the wise old man of the community. When a man who had been married happily for thirty years suddenly began fighting with his wife, where did the wife go for help? To my father. When a youngster rebelled and refused to obey his parents, where did the parents go for help? To my father. When a businessman suspected that his partner was cheating him, where did he go for help? To my father. He was friend, and counselor, and psychiatrist. All in all, he did everything that in later years welfare and social workers and bureaucracy would try to do. His were not acts of charity. They were acts of compassion and love.

So that was the atmosphere in which I grew up—filled with love and the love of life; filled with service to others and with respect for everyone; filled with old-fashioned virtues of hard work, fair play, and high ethical standards of conduct; filled with the kind of faith in oneself that overcomes adversity; and filled with the undying belief that as an American I could achieve *anything*.

Looking back, it seems as if the years of my boyhood rushed by—and all of a sudden it was graduation day at Stuyvesant High School, and I was faced with the problem of choosing my career.

2.

My first choice was influenced by a most unusual man. I knew him as Mr. Moscow, and I never did know his first name. He was one of my instructors in my senior year at Stuyvesant. He was a superb teacher, an inspirational teacher, and a pal to his students. He invited us to his home, played basketball with us, took us to the theater. He was genuinely interested in us. They seldom make that kind of teacher anymore.

Mr. Moscow taught creative writing. He brought out all my writing talent—talent that helped me later in life to write a syndicated column, and is helping me write this book. By the end of my senior year, I was convinced that there was only one career for me—writing. "So that's what you want to be, a writer?" my father said to me. "So let's examine the pros and cons." We did, and finally my father said, "What it amounts to, my boy, is that while writing is a fine and noble profession, you can't make a living from it." He was right; even today the majority of authors earn less than $5,000 a year. "Think about another career," my father advised me.

I examined my other talents. I had perfect grades in mathematics, chemistry, and physics, but in those days the bulk of jobs in those fields was in teaching, and I didn't see myself as a teacher for the rest of my life. But my excellence in math and science did qualify me for a career in which I could be out in the real world, not the academic world, and be making real money. That career was engineering. To become an engineer I had to go to college. That was the next phase of my life; and it was rich with lessons that helped me.

My first lesson came when it was time for me to register at college. It was now the time of the Great Depression. My father, who had been investing heavily in real estate, was wiped out. We were poor again. Tuition was several hundred dollars a year even in those days and we didn't have it, but I was a good enough student to win a Pulitzer scholarship, so there were no worries about tuition. I was now eligible to enter the Engineering School of Columbia University, an Ivy League school.

So now it is September 1934, and I'm seventeen years old, a poor Jewish boy from Brooklyn, and I'm standing in line in this posh, prestigious institution of higher learning, waiting to register for classes. I get to the front of the line, and there's this dignified lady sitting at a desk, and she looks over my credentials, and she looks up at me, and says, "You owe us $60." And I say, "What for?" And she says, "There are registration fees, and lab fees, and . . ." She goes on and on. I say, "I'm supposed to get in for nothing. I don't have $60." She says, "What do you have?" I say, "Just enough to get back to Brooklyn—a nickel." In those days the subway fare was only a nickel. "Just a nickel," she says, with a kind of little sneer, and then she says—and I'll never forget these words—"We don't want people like you at Columbia."

I'm still furious whenever I think back on it. She had decided I was a second-class citizen. That's not the American way. Every citizen is a first-class citizen. Every citizen has the right to an education if he or she earns that right. I had earned it: I had won a scholarship. In later life, I would never stand for anybody treating me, or anybody else, like a second-class citizen. But here I was still in my teens, in awe of just being at Columbia; I was flustered and frightened, and I didn't know how to assert myself. All I could think of saying was, "What am I supposed to do?" "Go uptown and register at CCNY," the registrar said to me. "That's the college for you."

CCNY, the City College of New York, in the '30s, and for many decades before, was one of the finest schools in the nation. Its entrance requirements were so high that only the smartest kids in town could get in. You had to have excellent high-school training in basic subjects like English, mathematics, physics, and languages, plus an average of 90 or more, before they would even consider you. Once admitted, you had to work hard—I mean, *really* work hard—because the competition from all those whiz kids was ferocious, and the professors expected nothing less than perfection. From the CCNY of those days came scores of Nobel Prize winners, authors, doctors, lawyers, business leaders, jurists, actors, playwrights, composers—men who contributed magnificently to the cultural, intellectual, and financial life of the city and the nation. Yet virtually every student at CCNY was a poor boy like myself. City, as the college was affectionately called, was free to any young man who lived in New York, provided he could meet the tough entrance requirements. I could. I enrolled for courses leading to a degree in civil engineering.

We did have to buy our own textbooks at City, and somehow, doing work here and there, I scraped up enough money to carry me through my freshman year. But in my sophomore year, the Depression was continuing and I couldn't find jobs anywhere; my father and mother had no money, everybody I knew was broke—and where, oh, where was I to get the money for the books to start the school year? I thought of Sam. Sam was an old attorney who lived in my neighborhood, the kind of attorney who has just about vanished. By today's standards he was a failure; he never made a great deal of money. He thought a lawyer's job was to help people, especially people who were in trouble, without making a fortune from them, and sometimes not taking anything at all.

I went to Sam, and I told him what was bothering me. "So how much do you need for these books?" Sam says. I tell him, "About $90." "So what's the problem?" Sam says with a big smile. He takes out his checkbook and writes me out a check for $100. "There," he says, holding it out to me. "Problem solved." "But Sam," I say, "I've still got three years of school, there's a Depression on, I don't know when I'll get some work—I don't know how I'll be able to pay you back." He's still holding out the check, and I'm not reaching out for it. "Take it," Sam says, "and I'll tell you how you'll pay me back."

I take it, and Sam then says something that has influenced every day of my life since. "I don't want any interest, not a penny," Sam says, "but this is going to be the hardest debt in the world to repay. The reason is, you're not going to pay me back in money. What you're going to do is, whenever anybody needs help, you're going to help. And every time you help, you're going to say to yourself, 'I'm paying Sam back.' Agreed?" "Agreed."

I have never stopped paying Sam back.

The lesson I learned from Sam is this: A good deed should have a multiplying effect. When you receive a good deed, you should pay it back with many good deeds. And the people who receive good deeds from you should do the same. If we all did this, what a fine world this would be.

Thanks to Sam I was able to continue at college. But the world was changing, and so were the students. Their noses weren't in their books entirely anymore. They were sniffing the winds of discontent that were howling in from Europe, and they smelled war. Adolf Hitler was Chancellor of the Third Reich, and anybody could see that if he were to get the *Lebensraum* he wanted for the German people, he would have to give the signal to his *Wehrmacht* to attack. And what would we, the students, do in case of war—would we fight or would we refuse? The campus was in turmoil. As for me, there was no doubt in my mind about what I would do.

At City, students could voluntarily enroll in the ROTC—the Reserve Officers Training Corps. Students who completed their course of training in the ROTC would, in the event of war, be automatically commissioned as second lieutenants in the U.S. Army. I felt America had been wonderful to me—where else in the world, for example, could I be trained to become an engineer free of charge with no strings attached?— and I owed my country a debt of gratitude. I enrolled in the ROTC.

I received my degree, found a job as a civil engineer, helped build the New York subway system; then Pearl Harbor exploded, and I was ready to do my bit. But to my disgust, others in the ROTC weren't. They didn't try to evade service, but they tried to get safe jobs in the Army. Many finagled their way into the Quartermaster Corps; no fighting there. And one kid used his father's influence to get a commission in the Judge Advocate's Office—the legal arm of the Army—that would never put him within a thousand miles of the front. But our nation, the nation I loved, was in a life-and-death struggle, and I had a passionate desire to fight and defeat the enemy. I elected to become a combat soldier, and I was commissioned as a lieutenant in the Infantry.

But the Army was short on civil engineers, and I was soon transferred to the Corps of Engineers. I was bitterly disappointed, but I realize today that the Army was right; war is fought in many ways, and a soldier should serve where he can do the most good. I served with distinction, and when the war ended I held the rank of captain, and I was asked to stay on as major. But it was over, we had won, I had done my duty, and while Army life as a civil engineer had its attractions, something was stirring inside of me, something that made me eager to see if I could succeed in the everyday competition of the civilian world. I set out to try.

By the time I was twenty-seven I had my own construction company in Philadelphia, and I had been personally responsible for over $100 million worth of construction. In terms of today's dollar that would be more than $1 billion. Friends said to me, "Hey, Bernie, you've got it made. Why don't you take it easy for the rest of your life?" But I had no idea of retiring at twenty-seven. I reviewed in my own mind just what I had learned: civil engineering, which had led to construction, and construction had led to real estate. So there were three areas which I knew a lot about, but they were all linked together by one field of knowledge about which I knew nothing—economics. And that lack of knowledge would hold me back from being even more successful than I was. "Beryl," my father had said, "you get ahead fast in America with education." So at twenty-seven, already a successful businessman, I decided to go back to school.

In the late '40s the Wharton School at the University of Pennsylvania was the best school of economics in the nation. I did well there even though I was carrying on a business while I went to school, and even though all the other students had sound basic grounding in economics, which made the competition tough. I received my master's degree, and went on to study for my Ph.D.

But my studies at Wharton didn't satisfy my thirst for more knowledge. I piled up expertise in other fields as well, not by going back to school but from life experience. (School is a necessary basis for learning; but without life experience what you learn in school is worthless.) I broadened my real estate know-how by giving up my own business for a while and taking a top executive position in the firm of the greatest real estate man I ever knew, Albert E. Greenfield. Then I taught myself to be an expert in other fields—finance, insurance, real estate appraisal, urban problems, city planning, purchasing, education, and investments.

My knowledge became so wide and so deep that I was asked to testify time after time as an expert witness in law cases. Very often decisions involving millions and millions of dollars rested on what I had to tell the jury, and how I handled myself under the attacks of the attorneys, which sometimes could be very vicious. Time after time, no matter what the attorneys did to try to tear down my testimony and discredit me, the jury would believe *me*. Honesty and knowledge and confidence have a way of making themselves felt—particularly when you're battling for what's right.

As the years passed, success piled on success. Honors were bestowed on me. I became a professor at Wharton part time, I was appointed to the Planning Commission of the City of Philadelphia, and I received many awards. But when somebody came to me with a problem and I tried to help (remember, I was always paying Sam back), I felt dissatisfied. I felt that even though my solution was technically correct, it was somehow wrong. Let me give you an example:

A man came to me at this time and said, "Dr. Meltzer, I've just inherited $20,000. I have a mortgage on my home at 6 percent. I can invest the $20,000 at 8 percent or pay off my mortgage. What shall I do?" The answer I gave was: "Since your mortgage only costs 6 percent, and you can get 8 percent on your money, invest your money and you'll be ahead by 2 percent."

The answer was logical, it made sense, but I knew in my heart there was something wrong. Then I thought of my father, the wise old man of the neighborhood, and I said to myself, "Would he have answered like a computer?"—because that was the way I was answering—"Or would he have answered like a human being?" Like a human being, of course! He would have looked behind the facts and figures, and found out what kind of person he was talking to, and tried to assess in his own mind what paying off the mortgage meant to the man *emotionally,* not simply what it meant in dollars and cents. My father had been a warm, compassionate, understanding person, and I would have to follow in his footsteps if I were to solve other people's problems as well as he did. I would have to learn to become a person like him—a human being.

I found the way. My father was deeply religious. I admit that as a youth, I had strayed and become skeptical. Once my rabbi told the class at the yeshiva (a religious school I attended after regular public-school hours) that God made stars as lights in the sky for the benefit of man. He placed them in the heavens after nightfall, and took them away at dawn. I got up in class and said, "You're wrong, rabbi," and I told him what stars really were according to the findings of astronomers. The rabbi was furious. He beat me with a stick and threw me out of the class. "Go away and never come back! You're an atheist! You're a *goy!*" But in middle age, I returned to religion. All religions are alike in that they all lead to God; and God's first commandment is always the same—"Love your fellow men as you would love yourself." When you follow God's commandment, you become a human being. Let me tell you why.

When you're motivated in your relations with other people by love, you're naturally compassionate and understanding, you're able to feel their problems with your heart. When that happens you just *cannot* treat people as if they were statistics being fed into a computer. You *cannot* just apply icy logic to their problems; you must temper reason with the warmth of life experience. You *cannot* just rely on your knowledge; you must use common sense. This is the way a human being solves other people's problems. And I became a human being.

Today if a man came to me with the problem of should he pay off the mortgage or invest the $20,000, I would first try to get to know the man. I would ask questions such as: How old are you? What kind of job do you have? How much have you been saving each week? And if I found out the man was close to sixty, had been a civil servant all his life, had put aside only $5 a week and watched his savings grow very, very slowly over the years, I wouldn't tell him to invest the $20,000 and not pay off the mortgage. I would tell him to pay off the mortgage. The reason is: Here is a man who prizes a sense of security over anything else. He has a secure job, he saved little by little but steadily over the years to obtain security, and he's getting on in years and he wants that feeling of security more than ever. And owning his home outright would give him the biggest sense of security he's ever had in his life.

When I give advice like this today, based on the human equation, and not on a mathematical equation, I often get calls from bankers who say to me, "You must be crazy! What kind of advice is that? Let him deposit his money in a CD at 14–15 percent, and on a 10 percent mortgage he'd be making 4 or 5 percent—that's $800 to $1,000. How can you tell a man not to become $800 to $1,000 richer?" Yes, he would be richer. But how much richer would he be in happiness? Not richer at all, but poorer. When a human being gives advice, the answers may sound crazy, but they're right.

Becoming a human being has also made my family life as warm and close as anyone could desire. I am married to the most beautiful woman in the world. She's a gifted singer, composer, and playwright, and is as dedicated as I am to helping others. Our family is big, seven children plus their husbands and wives; and although we all have separate lives, which is as it should be, our greatest joy is getting together and being with each other. Early in life, I learned that the family that sticks together holds the key to happiness; and my family life is proof of it.

Now you know my attitudes toward life, you know about my expertise in many fields, you know that I'm a human being. You know that when I solve a problem for somebody, I'm just being myself—the sum of everything you know about me. If you think your money problems can be solved by my just being myself, turn the pages. I hope you do, because I wrote this book to help you. After all, I still have a debt to pay to Sam.

PART I

*Solving Your Borrowing
Problems: How to Get
the Money You Need
When You Need It*

Chapter 1

We All Borrow

IS IT RIGHT TO BORROW?

Sometimes people say to me, knowing that my basic credo is that the old virtues are the best virtues, "Dr. Meltzer, if I want something shouldn't I save up until I have enough money to buy it?" The answer is, "Yes," if you feel uncomfortable about getting into debt. But you must temper the old-fashioned virtue of being free of debt with realistic financial life experience in the '80s. If you wanted to save up for many, many things most Americans find to be necessities, not luxuries, you would have to save up for a lifetime. The way things are, borrowing is something you just have to live with. It is also the best tool the average person can use to beat—and prosper from—inflation. Let me show you some instances where it makes sense to borrow.

1. BORROW TO GET GOING ON YOUR OWN.

Let's say you're young, you've got your first job, and you want to fly out of the nest and set up on your own. Well, why not? That's the human thing to do. But remember, this is the '80s, and everything you need to set up on your own has a price tag—a *big* price tag. Just add up some rough figures in your mind. How about rent? And a car? And furnishing and appliances? How about a stereo? Radio and TV? If you're a white-collar worker, you can't go around looking as sloppy as you did when you were at school, and clothes cost money. And so on. Unless you were born with a silver spoon in your mouth, you're not going to pay all those bills—and a lot more—from your weekly income. You're going to have to borrow, and in today's climate there's nothing wrong with it.

2. BORROW TO BUY A HOUSE.

Your singles days are over, the wedding bells have chimed, and now there are two of you with a single thought: Let's buy a house. Now, virtually no young couple can afford to buy a house for cash. Both of you are in your twenties, you're both working, you've been able to save up some money—but have you saved up $50,000, or $100,000, or more? We must think in terms of life experience; those are the prices that prevail, and they're going to go up, not down. If you waited to save $50,000, by the time you saved it, the house would cost $100,000; and if you waited until you saved $100,000, it would cost $200,000, and so on. You would never catch up, and you would never live in your own house. The only thing to do—and millions and millions of American families do it—is to borrow. Mortgages were invented for people like you.

3. BORROW TO START A FAMILY.

You know, Dr. Benjamin Spock is a wonderful man, and he tells you everything you need to know about bringing up kids. But there's one thing that kids need that he neglects to tell you about—money. Two *cannot* live as cheaply as one—so what do you expect when the number grows to three, or four, or five, or more? Kids are expensive from before they're born to the time they fly the coop. But just consider the starting costs: the baby's doctor, the hospital, the visiting nurse, the equipment you'll need, the baby clothes, the bedclothes, the special formulas . . . You know something? A baby is one of the big, big expenses of a lifetime. What are you going to do about it? Dig into your savings and leave yourself with little or nothing for a rainy day? The wise and sensible thing to do is borrow, and pay it back in small installments. For a few dollars a week, you can have the joy of children when *you* want them, and not when your *bank balance* says you can have them. That's one of the greatest joys in life. Don't deprive yourself of it.

4. BORROW TO EDUCATE YOUR KIDS.

More than ever your kids' future depends on education. There was a time when the most you had to plan for financially was college, graduate school, and professional school. You could rely on the public school systems to carry your kids through high school, and all you would have to pay if you lived in a suburban or rural area was school taxes, and you didn't have to pay anything at all if you lived in a big city. It's an unpleasant fact to face, but you have to face it—public schools are deteriorating, and the concerned parent is faced with the high costs of private schools. You want the best for your kids, so how do you raise the tuition for private school? You borrow. There's no other way a typical middle-class family can do it. And how do you finance higher education, with the costs going through the roof and heading for the stratosphere? Borrow.

I'm not advocating anything radical. Borrowing for the kids' higher education is the American way of life, and has been for a long time. And I predict that more and more parents will borrow to send their kids to private elementary and high schools. It's the trend of the future.

5. Borrow to Meet Big-Dollar Emergencies.

One of my associates was told by his doctor that he had to have immediate bypass surgery. The doctor said his life depended on it, and he couldn't put it off. My friend said, "What's it going to cost me?" The doctor said, "What are you worrying about? You're covered by health insurance, aren't you?" My friend said, "Yes, but still—what's it going to cost me?" The doctor said, "Oh, about $30,000, maybe $35,000." (I think it's outrageous to set that kind of price to save a man's life.) My friend said, "Well, I have health insurance, but it won't cover that." To pay the doctors and the hospital, he had to borrow. No other way out. When emergencies occur, and big dollars are the only solution, and you haven't the dollars, go ahead and borrow. That's one reason why banks and money stores are around—to help you get out of the jams of life.

And most important—

6. Borrow to Beat Inflation.

I have some sayings which people have begun to call "Meltzerisms"— pithy remarks which sum up a big truth in a little sentence or two. This book is going to be sprinkled with Meltzerisms. And here's the first one:

> **Meltzerism:**
> *If you need something, buy it today.*
> *Tomorrow it will cost you more.*

How much higher will prices go? When I give seminars around the country, I ask the audience, "How many of you think annual inflation in the '80s is going down to about 5 percent? Put up your hands."

Maybe one hand, two hands, go up. "How many think it will go up to 20 percent, 30 percent, or more?" A half-dozen or so hands go up. "And how many of you think inflation will stay around 10 percent?" A whole sea of hands goes up. That's good common sense, and I agree with it. You know what that means? The new sofa you have your eye on that sells for $2,000 today next year will sell for $2,200; the year after that for $2,420; the year after that for $2,662; the year after that for almost $3,000. Why wait?

Buy what you need today, then pay it back with dollars that are worth 10 percent less every year. Next year you'll be paying back only 90¢ on every dollar you owe; the year after that 81¢, and so on. So when you buy today you win in two ways: You save money on what you buy, and you save money on what you pay. Keep your eye open for sales, and you'll save *three* ways.

You can also borrow money to make investments. Should the investments pay off with returns higher than the rate of inflation, you gain two ways. Your profits keep you ahead of inflation while you pay for them with discounted inflation dollars.

ARE YOU A SAFE BORROWER?

How often does a wife or husband call me and complain, "We're in debt—over our heads in debt. How are we ever going to get out of it?" There are so many cases like that—I'm sure you know of some yourself —that you might well ask me how I can say go ahead and borrow. Last year about 150,000 families went into personal bankruptcy because the judges decided there was no way in the world they could pay off their debts even if they took the rest of their lifetimes to do it. So Bernard Meltzer must have his head examined when he says, "Borrowing is all right."

Not so. There are people who can borrow sanely and prudently and never even come close to overspending. I call those people *safe* borrowers. Most of the American people fall into that category. The people who get into serious debt trouble represent only about 1 percent of the population. That means on a statistical basis you only have one chance in a hundred of not being a safe borrower. But if you *are* that one in a hundred, you should no more use a credit card than an alcoholic should take a drink. Would you like to know if you are likely to become that one in a hundred? Just take this little test that I devised, and you'll find out in less than a minute.

7. THE SAFE BORROWER TEST.

Answer the following questions:

	YES	NO
When you dine out do you leave a bigger tip when you use a credit card than when you pay cash?	☐	☐
Do you borrow to meet current bills?	☐	☐
Do you pass up an item because of its price when you pay cash, but buy the item when you can use a credit card?	☐	☐
Do you gamble with the money you borrow? (Remember, playing the stock market is gambling.)	☐	☐
Are you inclined to buy an expensive item you don't really need because of the "easy payment" plan?	☐	☐
Do you use your charge accounts when you know you may not be able to meet the payments?	☐	☐
When you use your credit card do you feel like a big shot?	☐	☐
Do you spend more than 20 percent of your after-tax income on debt repayment?	☐	☐
Are you more likely to buy something on impulse with a credit card than with cash?	☐	☐
Do you use your credit card to go on buying binges?	☐	☐

If you answered any question Yes, the chances are you're not a safe borrower. The more questions you answered Yes, the more unsafe you are.

8. HOW TO BECOME A SAFE BORROWER.

I believe firmly that anybody can do anything he or she wants to do, that no matter what drawbacks you have, you can overcome them. I've done it and so can you. If that test shows you have a tendency to get into serious debt, or if you know from your own life experience that you do get into debt, or if you now are into debt, you can turn yourself around. The first thing to do is say to yourself, "I don't ever want to be in debt." Say it to yourself several times a day, and say it particularly every time you get the urge to overspend.

If you need a little psychological crutch to keep you from overspending, do this: Take a piece of paper or a card no bigger than a credit card and write on it what you're now paying out each month in debts. Let's say it's $170. Now figure out what your monthly income is after all deductions have been made. Take 15 percent of it—that's the absolute tops you can afford to spend on debt payment without getting into trouble, according to most debt counselors. Write that figure on a piece of paper in red. Let's say it's $175. You're already paying out $170 each month. The most you can add to that is $5 a month. So before you take out your credit card, take a look at those two numbers on the slip of paper, and make sure your new monthly debt payments won't exceed the number in red before you say, "Charge it!"

9. How to get out of heavy debt.

I'd like to get back to the question that's so often asked me—"We're in debt over our heads. How can we ever get out of it?" The best way to start is to go over your income and find out exactly what you're earning. I know so many people who kid themselves. "I'm earning $20,000 a year," they say. No, they're not. After they take off taxes, and pension plan, and union dues, and hospitalization, and whatnot, they're lucky if they're taking home $12,000. But they don't like to think of it that way —what a comedown, $12,000 instead of $20,000!—so what they do is spend as if they really were making $20,000. So be realistic. Figure out what your *real* income is each month. And learn to live with the truth.

Now step two is going to be just as painful. What you have to do is sit down with a pencil and paper and figure out just what your expenses are each month. If I were a betting man—which I'm not; I think betting is just for losers—I'd bet that *you* don't know what your expenses really are. I'll prove it. Jot down right here what you *think* your monthly expenses are: ——

Now get that pencil and paper and on one side write in a column: mortgage (or rent), utilities, taxes not deducted from your paycheck, food, clothing, transportation, car maintenance, and anything else you can think of, including birthday presents and money you put aside for Christmas and vacation time. Then next to each item, pencil in the actual monthly cost. Add up all the cost figures, and jot down the total here: ——

Compare it with the figure you wrote down previously. Did I win the bet?

You probably found out that you're spending more each month than you thought. But now you know the *real* figure. Subtract it from your *real* income. The difference is what you have to pay your debts. Let's say it's $200. Now compare that figure with the amount of debts you have to pay. Say they amount up to $300. There's no way you can pay $300 with $200. But you can pay off your debts if you reduce your monthly debt load to $200 or less. And the way you do that is, you go to the people you owe money to, and you say, "Look, here are the facts and figures"—and you show what your real income is and what your real expenses are—"and I'll pay you off, if you just let me reduce my payments by one third each month." Sure, they'll say yes. They want to get paid, and if that's the only way you can pay them, fine! Sometimes getting out of heavy debt is easier than you think.

10. BANKRUPTCY IS THE LAST RESORT.

I had a couple come to me, and they said something like this. "Dr. Meltzer, we've followed your advice, and we've figured out our real monthly income, and we've figured out our real monthly expenses, and the amount of surplus money we have after we pay expenses is zero. In fact, it's a minus figure. And we're up to our ears in debt. What shall we do?" That couple was in a bad situation, but weren't any worse off than a lot of people you and I know. There was no way they could pay their debts; and in the old days they would have been put in jail for it—debtor's prison. But this is a wonderful compassionate country. There are laws passed by Congress which permit you to wipe out your debts and start all over again with a clean slate. So I advised this couple to take advantage of the laws. These laws are called bankruptcy laws, and they should only be used when there's nothing else you can do to get out of debt.

You can file for bankruptcy yourself by going to the clerk of your Bankruptcy Court, and asking what forms to fill out and what to do with them after you've filled them out. But it's safest to get a lawyer who knows something about the bankruptcy laws. Some of these new legal clinics, like Jacoby and Meyers, will handle your petition for you at bargain prices. What you need a good lawyer for, besides handling all the details and red tape which could drive you crazy, is to tell you which of the two kinds of bankruptcy law is best for you.

One kind is called Chapter 11 of the Bankruptcy Law, or simply Chapter 11; and the other kind is called Chapter 13 of the Bankruptcy Law, or simply Chapter 13. No matter which chapter you file for, the moment you file, your creditors are forbidden by law to harass you in any way. If they even call you on the phone and say "How do you do?" the Court will come down on them like a ton of bricks. They're not allowed to get in touch with you in any way. So filing for bankruptcy does one good thing fast—it gets the creditors off your back.

When you file for Chapter 11, you and your lawyer figure out your real monthly expenses just as I told you to do, and you submit your balance sheet to the Court. The Court will look it over, and maybe it will see some way of your squeezing out something for your creditors. Maybe 10¢ on each dollar you owe or maybe 5¢. Your creditors don't have to agree, because the Court says to them, "You take it, or else." The Court gives you a long time to pay it off, so it's not too hard on you.

When you file for Chapter 13, it's because you and your lawyer agree that the debt structure is so high that in no way can you repay it. Based upon the facts in the case, the Court may scale down the level so that you are now capable of repaying. For example, you may owe $10,000, but all you can repay based upon your income is $3,000; therefore the Court will scale your debt down to that level. If your income is so low, or you have none, the Court may forgive the entire debt.

You'll feel relieved, but do you think it's going to make you feel happy? From my life experience with many bankrupts over the years, I know bankruptcy can be a shattering emotional experience. You're telling your kids to grow up and be a responsible human being, and here *you* are reneging on your debts. Do you think that makes you feel good? Far from it. Deep in your heart you know it's morally wrong to run up debts and not pay them. Unless there are circumstances beyond your control, like losing your job or a catastrophic illness, going into bankruptcy is no better than stealing. You won't be able to wash the feeling of shame off you for years, and as a practical matter your credit is ruined for a long, long time. That's why I say, use the bankruptcy law to protect yourself when your back is up against the wall—after all, it's a right granted you by the U.S. Congress—but use it only as a last resort.

BERNARD MELTZER'S ADVICE ON BORROWING

In the world we live in, borrowing is morally right and financially sound when you are a safe borrower and you're borrowing for the right purpose.

Chapter 2

Borrowing at Banks

ARE THERE DIFFERENT WAYS TO BORROW AT BANKS?

There certainly are. As a consumer you can get cash in six different ways. And besides that, you can get automobile loans, mortgage loans, home improvement loans, federally guaranteed student loans, and education loans.

11. CASH LOANS.

What I'm going to tell you about in this section is what kind of cash loans are available, and how much cash you can expect from each kind of loan. Later on, I'm going to tell you what the loans cost.

• *Signature loans.* All you have to do is sign a form, which is actually an IOU, a pledge that you'll pay back, and if you're credit-worthy—which means if the computer thinks you can and will pay the loan back—you can have a check, or cash deposited to your account, in twenty-four hours. Usually the most you can get is $15,000.

• *Secured loans.* What you have to do is put up some of your assets—things you own—as security in case you can't pay back what you borrowed. But banks won't accept *any* kind of assets. They won't take your TV set as security, for example, or your electric guitar. What they'll take are gilt-edged stocks and bonds, your savings account, or your CDs (certificate of deposits).

It's easy to see why you would want to borrow against a CD. CDs pay as much as three times more than passbook accounts, but they tie your money up for long periods of time—six months to several years in most cases. Sometimes you can withdraw funds before maturity—that's the date when the bank gives you back what you invested plus interest— but there are severe penalties; you may lose as much as two-thirds of the interest you've earned. And sometimes there's no way a bank will permit you to withdraw your money before maturity. So once you put your money in most CDs, forget about it until the maturity date. But what happens if between the time you've made your investment and maturity date you need some or all of the cash you invested? You simply go to the bank and borrow, putting up your CDs as security. It's one of the cheapest ways to borrow, because if you're paying, say, 18 percent on the loan, you're still earning, say, 15 percent on your CDs, so what you're paying for the money is only 3 percent. And at some banks on some CDs, you only pay 16 percent on the loan, which brings the cost of your money down to 1 percent. Let me tell you, that's a bargain.

Same thing with passbook loans. I had a lady call me up and say, "Dr. Meltzer, I know it makes good horse sense to borrow on CDs, but it makes no sense at all to borrow on passbook accounts. When I need money, I just draw it out of my account and I don't pay a cent of interest." I said to this woman, "How much do you draw out?" She said, "Maybe $100 . . . maybe $200." I said, "No more than that?" She said, "Oh, no!" I said, "And you put it back as soon as you can?" She said, "Oh, yes! I don't like to see my balance shrink." I said, "How much do you have in your account?" She said, "About $5,000. It's my nest egg." I said, "Does it make you feel secure to have $5,000 in your account?" She said, "It certainly does. It would be like I didn't have a roof on my house if it wasn't there." I said, "Suppose you had a big expense, say $4,000, how would you feel about drawing that amount out?" "It would be terrible. I'd feel awful." "All right," I said, "what you should do is as follows. . . ."

And I told her *not* to take the $4,000 out, but to take out a $4,000 loan instead. Then her $5,000 would be intact, and she would be collecting interest on it while she was repaying the loan. And I told her that passbook loans are cheaper than personal loans, so she would be paying perhaps 12 percent for the loan instead of say 18 percent for a personal loan; and in addition to that she would be earning say 5¼ percent on her passbook loan, so her *actual* cost for the loan would be only 6¾ percent, which is still pretty cheap. "Thank you, Dr. Meltzer, for clearing that up," she said. "In that case, a passbook loan makes good horse sense."

• *Ready credit.*   Years and years ago when banking was just getting started in this country, a businessman might have said to his partner,

"We're going to need so-and-so much money for the payroll every week, and in a few weeks from now we're going to have to pay the steel company, and in two months we'll have to pay for that shipment of bauxite, and it's a darn nuisance to have to go to the bank every time we need dollars, and Jim Fitch down at the bank told me confidentially it costs them money to process a lot of small loans instead of one big one. So Jim made this proposal to me:

" 'Look, about $100,000 is going to cover you for the year. We'll put it aside for you, and while we're holding it, you don't have to pay a cent of interest on it. But whenever you need the money—for your payroll, to pay your suppliers, anything at all connected with your business—why, you just come around and the money is yours. Then, and only then, do you start paying interest on it. And when you've paid off what you've borrowed—any sum under $100,000—then your credit line goes back to $100,000 again.' "

And that's the way the "credit line" was born. The very simple idea behind it is that the bank makes a loan *in advance of the borrower's need*. It was a great banking innovation. These days the credit line is offered to consumers as well as businessmen.

One way you can get a line of credit is through a plan called "ready credit." The way it works is as follows. The bank opens a checking account for you, only you don't deposit a cent in it. But the bank puts as much as $5,000 in it. That's your credit line. When you want to use the money, you just write a check. You can write checks for cash, or to pay your bills, or for any other purpose.

Meltzerism:
It's nice to have a loan waiting for you when it costs you nothing while it's waiting.

• *Overdraft loans.* This is a spinoff of ready credit. Instead of the bank depositing money for you in a separate checking account, it deposits it in your own account. On the average, $2,000 is the most the bank will deposit. This is the way it works:

Say you have a balance of $197.27 in your account, and you have bills amounting to $500 which must be paid. Under ordinary circumstances if you wrote checks for $500, many of them would bounce. But with that extra $2,000 the bank deposited in your account, you can write those checks and they'll be honored. In this case, you would draw on your line of credit for $302.73—which is the difference between $500 and $197.27—and you'd start paying interest on that amount.

Your credit line would then be down to $1697.27, but it would go back to $2,000 when you deposited $302.73 into your account, at which time you would pay no further interest.

Why is it called an overdraft loan? In banker's language an overdraft means writing a check on your account for more than the amount of your deposits in it. That's what you do when you write yourself an overdraft loan.

• *Credit card loans* are another extension of the line-of-credit idea. You'll notice that when you're issued a bank credit card—Visa or MasterCharge—you get a written notice from the issuing bank that your credit line is $500 or $1,000 or anything up to $2,000 on the average. That means you can charge anything up to that amount. If your balance goes over that amount, the bank will notify shopkeepers and restaurant owners not to accept your card.

A young man called me, and he said, "I've had a bank credit card for years, and I never knew I could draw cash on it." It's a well-kept secret. But you can draw cash up to the amount of your credit line. If your credit line is $2,000, and you've run up no charges, you can walk into any bank honoring your card, and walk out with $2,000 in cash. (There are exceptions. Check with your bank.) Getting a credit card loan is the easiest and simplest way of getting a loan.

"Isn't there something wrong about using credit cards?" I'm asked time and time again. I'll get into that subject later on in the book when I talk to you about buying. But for now all I'll say is, I carry credit cards and I use them.

• *Second mortgages.* One of the questions I'm asked very frequently by young people is, "What's the difference between a first mortgage and a second mortgage?" Before I answer that I'd like to make a brief comment on our school system. What do they teach youngsters to prepare them for life? Nothing very practical. I knew a Phi Beta Kappa who got out of a school and didn't know how to write a check. I think it's deplorable. And before we start pouring more and more money into our schools, we should stop and say, "What are they teaching?" Yes, I think a man or woman should start adulthood with a knowledge of the basic economic facts of life. One reason why I wrote this book is that they're not taught this. (The major reason, as you already know, is to help people of all ages solve their money problems.) I think it's a crying shame that young people, or anybody who comes out of our educational system, should not know the answers to simple financial questions, because those answers are sure to affect their future and their happiness.

To get back to the question. A first mortgage is a way of financing your home. The money you get goes for the purchase of your home, nothing else. You don't even see the money. It goes from the bank right to the seller. I want to repeat, you can't do anything with your mortgage money except pay for your home. To understand what a second mortgage is, you have to first understand what "equity" means. The best way of explaining it is with an example. You buy a home, and you put down $10,000. But the home costs $50,000. The other $40,000 is raised with a first mortgage. So the holder of the first mortgage, the bank in this case, owns 80 percent of your home (you get that figure by dividing $40,000 by $50,000) and you own the remaining 20 percent. What you own is your equity. As you pay off the mortgage year by year your equity increases. In the last year of the mortgage, your equity can go up to 90 or 95 percent or more. When you pay off the mortgage in full, your equity is 100 percent. Now a *second* mortgage is a loan secured by your equity in your home. You're paid in cash, and you can use the money in any way you wish.

Inflation of home values has made the second mortgage a very popular way of raising large sums of cash. I'll show you why. One couple I know bought their house nineteen years ago for $25,000. They have $2,500 remaining on their mortgage, so one might think their equity is now 90 percent. But in those nineteen years the value of their home has gone up to $125,000. Their equity is now not 90 percent of $25,000 but 98 percent of $125,000! The bank's equity is only $2,500, or 2 percent of $125,000. Most banks will subtract what's still owed on the first mortgage, in this case $2,500, then give a second mortgage of up to 75 percent of what remains. This couple could get a second mortgage for as much as $91,875—and that's a lot of cash!

Well, those are the six ways you can borrow cash from a bank. Now let's look at some of the other kinds of loans banks offer.

12. LOANS FOR SPECIFIC PURPOSES.

These are not like cash loans in that the borrower is required to use the money for one thing and one thing only.

• *Mortgage loans* are the way most homes—houses, condos, co-ops, and even mobile homes—are financed. We'll go into mortgages in great detail in Part II, Solving Your Buying Problems.

• *Home improvement loans.* You get the money in cash, but under the terms of the loan it's earmarked for specific home improvements. It's a violation of your loan agreement if you use the cash for anything else.

• *Automobile loans.* Almost every adult American has had experience with these loans. Usually your car dealer makes all the arrangements for you. I'll have a lot more to say about auto loans in Part II, Solving Your Buying Problems.

• *Education loans.* I've never known anybody to have any difficulty getting an education loan, especially when the loan is guaranteed by the federal government. Your best guide to getting an education loan for your kids is the bursar of the school or college they're attending. Often a school or college has a tie-in with a specific bank, in which case the bursar's office will handle all the arrangements for you.

CAN YOU GET ALL KINDS OF CONSUMER LOANS AT EVERY BANK?

There are four kinds of banks, and they're alike in only one respect—they all accept deposits, and lend out the deposits at interest to make money. In the years ahead we're going to see the different kinds of banks become more and more alike, but right now they're different in a number of ways. Up to recently you couldn't get all kinds of consumer loans in all four kinds of banks. But now you can. Let's take a look at—

13. THE FOUR KINDS OF BANKS.

I'm going to tell you what each of them are and what kind of loans you can get from them. Later on, I'll tell you what these loans will cost you.

• *The commercial bank.* It's the oldest kind of bank in the country, and it goes way back to colonial days. It was founded to serve the business community. Even these days, if you're running a business you'll prefer to deal with a commercial bank. But in recent years, commercial banks have been spreading their wings, and they've gone all out to attract the consumer trade. You've seen the full-page ads in the newspapers, and the expensive commercials on radio and TV. In a commercial bank you can get every kind of consumer loan available.

• *The savings bank* originated back in the 1880s to serve the needs of little guys—workers, farmers, small-business men, lawyers, accountants, doctors (yes, doctors *were* little guys in those days), and so on. The banks were formed for the mutual interest of everybody concerned, so even today savings banks are called "mutual savings banks." But the word "mutual" has become meaningless. Savings banks are in business to make money, just as any other business is. You'll find savings banks in only seventeen states, and their practices differ not only from state to state, but from bank to bank. Consumer loans, except for first mortgages, are harder to get at savings banks than at commercial banks.

• *Savings and loan associations.* They began because people back in the early part of the nineteenth century didn't have enough money to build their own homes, particularly in the East. Commercial banks weren't interested in putting up mortgages for the little guy. Savings banks hadn't been formed yet. So bankers got the people who couldn't afford their own homes together and said, "Let's form an association. And the purpose of the association will be this—to make mortgage loans." Where were they going to get the money for the loans? From the deposits of the members of the association. And that's how they got the name "savings and loan associations." Today there are 5,000 or so savings and loan associations in the country, and they supply the bulk of the nation's mortgages. If you're looking for a first mortgage, a savings and loan association is a good place to go. But you'll get other types of consumer loans easier at commercial banks.

• *Credit unions.* So far of the three kinds of banks I've talked about, one, the commercial bank, was set up basically for business, and the other two, the savings bank and the savings and loan association, for the consumer. Now I'm going to tell you about the credit union—a bank set up *by* consumers *for* consumers. Here's what they're all about:

A credit union has nothing to do with a labor union (although labor unions can form credit unions). It's a *union* of people—that is to say, an organization—devoted to making loans, in other words extending *credit*. So put "union" and "credit" together, and you get "credit union." But to form a credit union the people who get together must have a common interest. That means you must belong to the same lodge, or work together in the same company, or go to the same church, and so on.

The credit union works, like all banks, on the deposit system. The members of a credit union deposit their savings into it, the savings are invested, and loans are made on the basis of the savings and the profits from the investments. Just how much money you can get on each type of consumer loan depends on the individual credit union. All loans are easy to get—far easier than at any other type of bank. But you can't get *any* kind of loan from a credit union unless you're a member. For details on setting up your own credit union, write CUNA, P.O. Box 431, Madison, WI 53701.

CAN YOU GET LOANS FROM PLACES OTHER THAN BANKS?

Yes, you can. The worst way to get loans, in my opinion, is from loan sharks and unloving relatives. When a loan shark says to you, "Seven and a half for five," he means he'll give you $5 if you return $7.50 the next week. And he's a nice guy. He says, "If you ain't got the five bucks, just give me back the two and a half. And give me back the two and a half every week until you can come up with the five bucks too." Some nice guy! You know what annual interest you're paying? Two thousand six hundred percent!

I also want you to know that although you don't sign anything, and you don't put up anything as security, it's a secured loan. It's secured with your limbs, your eyes, your face, and sometimes your life. A loan shark is likely to say to a customer who can't get up the interest payment, "I'm a nice guy, and I don't wanna see you hurt. But, buddy, maybe you're gonna walk across the street and a car's gonna run into you. I sure would be sorry to see that happen."

When you borrow from unloving relatives, the injury you suffer is emotional. I've had many, many people say to me, "My sister"—or brother, or son, or daughter, or any kind of relative—"wants to borrow $1,000. What shall I do?" I ask, "Can you afford it?" They say, "Yes." I say, "Then what's your problem?" And they answer, "In the first place, how can I charge them interest? So even if I do get the money back, I'll be losing interest on it. And second, I don't know whether I'll ever get the money back." I say, "If that's the way you feel, say no."

But many of them say yes anyhow. They begrudge you the money. They don't come out and say so, but they make you feel it in a thousand small ways. What kind of relationship is that?

On the other hand, in a loving family everybody wants to help. I know a case where this woman said to her sister, "I need $1,000 desperately. Will you take my silverware as collateral?" "Here's a check for the $1,000," the sister answered, "and whoever heard of collateral among sisters? Keep the silverware, and when you can pay me, pay me, and if you can't, you can't." This is one of those times when the human equation far outweighs the mathematical equation when it comes to money.

BERNARD MELTZER'S ADVICE
ON BORROWING FROM RELATIVES

Don't hesitate to borrow when there's a loving relationship. Then the money is given freely, and the loving relationship continues. When there's no loving relationship, don't borrow.

"Should I borrow from my friends?" I'm often asked. That's a question of what kind of friends they are. If they're acquaintances or "office friends," you'll be embarrassing them and you'll be embarrassing yourself. Just as with unloving relatives, if they don't lend you the money, you resent it; and if they do, they resent it. With real friends, it's a different story. They have your interest at heart, and it's all right to ask; and if they can, they'll give.

BERNARD MELTZER'S ADVICE
ON BORROWING FROM FRIENDS

When you borrow from friends, make it a business proposition. Put it on paper, pay interest, and pay it back when it's due. That way you'll stay friends.

And while we're talking about borrowing in a businesslike fashion, let's look in now at—

Chapter 3

Places Other Than Banks
Where You Can Borrow Money

As I said before, you have to look at borrowing realistically in relation to life experience in the '80s. Most of us don't borrow because we've mismanaged our money and we *have* to borrow. Most of us borrow to get the things we want which we couldn't get otherwise—and some of those things which were considered luxuries not so long ago are now necessities. And some of us borrow to keep ourselves healthy and even to save our lives—the cost of health care has become outrageously unreasonable. We borrow in most cases to make our lives more comfortable, more serene, happier. So don't look at borrowing in the old-fashioned sense, as something you only do when your back's against the wall. Look at it in the modern sense as using money to buy a better life for yourself while you beat inflation.

Now, money is a commodity like anything else. It's bought and it's sold. You sell money to the banks when you deposit it with them. They pay you for the use of your money. They call the payment "interest"—but by any name it's a profit to you for selling them money. On the other hand, the banks sell money to you when they make you a loan. For the use of that money, you pay the banks interest. So you can look at the banks as money merchants, buying and selling money. But there are other money merchants who don't buy money from you; they just sell it to you. Let's take a look at them.

14. A LIST OF MONEY LENDERS (MONEY SELLERS).

• *Second mortgage companies.* Second mortgages are very profitable, and many kinds of financial institutions other than banks have entered the field. They don't call themselves "second mortgage" companies, but go by a variety of names. Often the word "funding" appears in their titles. Some are known simply as "money stores." The giant small loan companies, Household International, Inc. (formerly Household Finance), and Beneficial Corporation, recently moved into the second mortgage business. Individuals with a good deal of money to invest now invest it in second mortgages (look for their names in the Yellow Pages under "Mortgages"). You can expect no more than 75 percent of equity from any second mortgage company.

• *Security brokers.* "Margin" means buying securities on credit (and we'll go into that in detail when we get to Part II, Solving Your Buying Problems, and brokers have offered margin for years. Something new has happened in recent years, and some brokers are now offering cash instead of credit. For example, if you have a portfolio worth $100,000, they'll offer you up to 50 percent of it in cash. It's an easy way for the broker to make extra dollars, and it's an easy way for you to get cash when you need it.

• *Credit card companies.* By that I don't mean Visa and MasterCharge; they're bank credit card companies, and I've already told you how you can raise cash with your bank cards. When I say credit card companies I mean the T&E (travel and expense) card companies—American Express, Carte Blanche, and Diner's Club, the glamour card companies. The surprising part about the cards of these companies is, you can't raise cash on two of them, and on the other the cash you can raise is no more than at most banks and less than at some. Carte Blanche will not give you cash, and neither will Diner's Club. If you're out of the country, though, Diner's Club will give you $500, then another $500 after a week. You can get cash only on an American Express Gold Card, not a regular card, and then only for up to $2,000. Some banks, like Manufacturers Hanover in New York, allow cash loans of up to $25,000 on their MasterCharge.

• *Life insurance companies.* Not infrequently, a man will come to me and say, "I've had a life insurance policy for twenty years, and I understand I can borrow money on it. What do you advise?" I say, "Do you need the money?" He says, "Yes." I say, "Do you understand that if you should die tomorrow, the amount you borrow will be deducted from what your widow gets?" He says, "I guess I didn't realize that." I say, "Do you understand that if you don't pay back the loan, the amount you borrowed plus accrued interest will be deducted from the amount your widow gets?" He says, "I hadn't thought about that either." I say, "Understanding those drawbacks, do you still want to take the loan?" He says, "I'm not going to drop dead tomorrow, because I'm in perfect health. And my wife's not going to lose anything, because I intend to pay the loan back as fast as I can. Now what's your advice, Dr. Meltzer?" "Take it."

The reason why I say take it is that it's probably the least expensive kind of loan you can get, unless you're putting up high-interest CDs as security. There's a clause in most life insurance policies—a policy is really a contract between you and the insurance company—which states you can borrow against the "cash value" of the policy; and if it's an old policy the interest rate can be as low as 4 percent. What "cash value" means is this: Each year you pay the insurance company a certain amount of money in premiums. The insurance company deducts expenses and profits from it, and what's left is your cash value. The cash value grows from year to year; and in most life insurance policies there's a chart showing you how it grows, so at any year you know exactly what your cash value is.

When you borrow from an insurance company you can get up to 95 percent of your cash value. It's easy to get the money, because all you have to do is send the company a letter. In two weeks or sooner, the company will send you a check.

One caller complained that he wanted to get a life insurance loan, and the insurance company said no way. I said to the man, "What kind of a policy do you have—term or whole life?" And sure enough, it was term. You can't get a loan on term insurance because it does not build a cash value. That's one reason term insurance is so cheap compared to whole life. (Term insurance is terminated after a specified number of years—say ten years or twenty years. Whole life means you have your policy during your whole life.) The only kind of policy you can borrow against is a whole life policy. That could be a consideration when you're thinking of which kind of policy is right for you.

• *Small loan companies,* which are also known as consumer loan companies, personal finance companies, and finance companies, are restricted by state laws to making loans only up to $2,500. There are a lot of people who don't make too much money and who need a small loan from time to time to buy a new piece of furniture or a TV or a vacation, and you can't get that kind of loan at a bank. Most banks won't even look at you if you want to borrow less than $3,000. So the small loan companies do a good and needed job for a lot of people.

If your credit's good, they'll give you a signature loan. And if it's not so good, they'll ask you to put up your household furniture as collateral. That's called a "chattel mortgage." You can also get auto loans and second mortgages at a small loan company.

• *Industrial loan companies* were set up to service industrial—blue-collar—workers. They offer all the services of a small loan company, but the maximums on their loans are higher—$5,000, for example, on a personal loan rather than $2,500.

• *Your employer.* "Dr. Meltzer, should I borrow from my employer?" is a question that comes up from time to time. "Do you mean you want an advance on salary?" I ask. If the answer is yes, I say, "This is not the kind of question that can be answered by a mathematical equation. On an advance in salary, your boss isn't going to charge you interest, so that's the cheapest loan you can make outside of one from your family. So mathematically, the answer should be, 'Go ahead and get the advance.' But," I go on, "let's take into consideration the life situation. What kind of a person is your boss? Will he think less of you when you ask for an advance? Will it hurt your chances of advancement? If you can be hurt in any way by asking for the advance—even though it costs you nothing in interest—don't ask for it. And suppose your boss *is* a nice guy, and you decide it's okay to take an advance—what about *you?* Will you be strapped on the next payday when the advance comes out of your check? Will you have enough money to get through to the next payday? You know yourself better than anyone. *You* decide whether an advance is going to hurt you or help you."

On the other hand, some companies have departments set up to handle employee loans. This is done on a strict business basis. You get the loan—often as high as six months' salary—and you pay the company interest on it. The company is happy to do it for you because it's making money, and there's no stigma attached to it at all. You pay back with small salary deductions over a long period, so you really don't feel it.

• *Executive loan services.*   Funny thing, the higher-salaried you are, the easier it is to get a loan—and a big one—from your employer. If you're earning $500,000 or more a year, and you have a chance to make a killing in an investment, and you need $100,000 or $200,000, the chances are your company will negotiate a loan with you. Ballplayers sometimes have loan agreements written into their contracts. But if you're in middle management and you're earning about $50,000 or $60,000, upper management looks on a loan request as a weakness. What you do then, if you need up to $25,000, is go to a bank or a second mortgage company; or you can get the money you need by mail from an executive loan service.

These services advertise in trade magazines and in airline magazines.

How they operate is as follows: You apply for a loan by phone, they send you an application form and ask you to provide proof of your salary—your WC-2 form, for example—and if you have a good credit rating and a history of job stability, they'll let you have your money by return mail. There used to be about twenty of these services in the nation offering loans by mail. But some of them have discontinued their mail service. For executive loan services near you, look for their ads in the Yellow Pages under "Loans."

• *Pawnshops.*   There are a lot of us who can't get a loan for a lot of reasons—credit is bad, you're temporarily out of work, your credit ceiling has been reached, and so on. When that happens you think about pawning something, and the question that's put to me is, "I've never been to a pawnshop before in my life. Should I go?" Once again, you have to weigh the mathematical equation with the human equation.

Let's take the mathematical equation first. When you put something into hock, you'll have to leave it with the pawnbroker until you've paid off the loan. Will you be happy without your color TV, or your wristwatch, or your diamond ring? Maybe not, so that's a negative factor in the equation. Here's another: The pawnbroker will almost never give you more than 25 percent of the retail value of whatever it is you're hocking. That's very little. So if you want to raise $2,000, you'll have to come in with an item worth $8,000 or more. Do you *own* such an item? So from a mathematical standpoint—and that's the standpoint most consumer experts take—you should be told to stay away from the pawnshop.

Now let's take the human equation. Let's say you're a freelance writer, and you want to take a vacation for a month. You have a brand-new typewriter worth about $800 that will be sitting around doing nothing for a month, and you could use $200 to pay your transportation costs, because you don't have it, and won't have it until your royalty check comes in next month. No chance of your getting a loan anywhere else. There's no reason why you shouldn't hock your typewriter until you come back. Anytime you're in a situation where the pawnshop is the only solution to your loan problem, don't pass it by just because consumer experts say you should. Just use your head, and take advantage of the service pawnshops have to offer.

Now you know about banks and all the other places where you can make loans. Let's now see how much it will cost you to make loans in all kinds of money stores, and what the advantages and disadvantages of each kind of store are.

Chapter 4

The Cost of Borrowing

WHERE'S THE BEST PLACE TO BORROW MONEY?

Now if I were a regular consumer expert, I would draw up a chart, and in one column I would put down the names of all the places you can borrow from, and in a parallel column I would put down opposite each name the interest you're charged for each kind of loan. Then I would say, "Run your finger down the interest column, and when you find the cheapest interest, that's the place to get your loan." But life isn't that simple. There are a lot of advantages and disadvantages associated with each kind of moneylender that must be considered. And then when you've considered the interest, *and* the advantages and disadvantages, you must decide for yourself which moneylender suits you best.

15. EVALUATING MONEYLENDING SOURCES.

In evaluating moneylending sources, I'm going to take the commercial bank as a standard—not because it's necessarily the best source for you, but because I have to set up some sort of standard against which I can assess the other sources. The things I'm going to measure for each money source are interest rates, length of repayment, advantages, and disadvantages.

But before I begin I want to say a word about interest rates. They're not going to be stable as the '80s roll on. On the whole, I predict, they'll rise. But they won't rise in a straight line; they'll zigzag. Take second mortgage rates as an example. In 1977 they were 15 percent. In June

1980, they jumped to 18 percent. In October of the same year, they fell to 15 percent again. And at the time this book went to press, they were up to 19 percent. So to quote accurate percentage figures, this book would have to be revised every few months. To get around that here's what I've done; I've made all figures except those of the commercial bank comparative, based on the commercial bank's figures as standard. For example, I'll say interest rates at credit unions are at least ¼ percent lower than at commercial banks. So whatever the interest rate at commercial banks is on the day you read this book, you'll know that interest rates at credit unions are about ¼ percent lower. Let's say you put down the book and you look at the financial page of your newspaper, and it says interest rates at commercial banks for consumer loans are 21.5 percent; then you'll know at once that the rates at your credit union will be just about 21.25 percent.

• *Evaluating commercial banks.* At the time this book went to press, commercial banks were charging 18 to 21 percent for signature, overdraft, and credit card loans; 16 to 19 percent on secured loans; and 19 percent on second mortgages. On auto loans for new cars, the interest rate was 10 to 14 percent, and on used cars, 12 to 18 percent; on mortgage loans, 17 percent; on home improvement loans, 15 to 17 percent; and on educational loans, 12 percent if they were not government-guaranteed, and 8 percent if they were. Passbook and CD loans were still a bargain at 12 percent because the money in your passbooks and CDs was earning money for you, sharply reducing the cost of the loan.

On signature and secured loans, you can get one to three years to repay; that's the same amount of time you can get to repay overdraft and credit card loans. On a first mortgage you get from thirty to thirty-five years, and on a second mortgage from three to ten years. You get five to ten years on a home improvement loan. On educational loans, you get up to ten years after graduation. On auto loans, three to five years. And on passbook and CD loans, three to five years.

Important: I know all these figures are boring, and I don't expect you to read through them for fun. But when you're thinking of a loan and you want some idea of what it will cost you, all you have to do is look back on these pages and you'll have some guidelines. One thing is certain—borrowing is expensive, and over the long run it's not going to get any cheaper. So if you're thinking of getting a loan for something you don't really need, just look at those figures, and think it over.

Now let's get on with a look at the advantages and disadvantages of dealing with a commercial bank. I hear this question frequently: "Commercial banks are for business, and I'm an individual. Won't I get lost in a commercial bank?" No, why should you? Banks of all types are in fierce competition with each other for every dollar they can get. It would be childish to pretend you're as important to a bank as a business account in the millions, but they need your dollars too—and the dollars of thousands like you. You won't get lost in a commercial bank for two reasons: The consumer division is well-organized and efficient; and the computer treats you as well as it treats anybody else. Besides, commercial banks offer all sorts of services which other banks may not offer, such as round-the-clock withdrawal and deposit privileges; special divisions for working women, professionals, and senior citizens; and a large number of branches you can use at your convenience. True, commercial banks tend to be more impersonal than other banks, but in many cases impersonality is an advantage—you can transact your bank business fast and without diversions. Doing business with a commercial bank can be a pleasurable experience.

So far as getting personal loans from this kind of bank, it's simple—all you do is fill out a form and put the form in the mail. You don't have to go in and see a loan officer; he or she doesn't look you up and down; you don't have to try to make an impression; there's no cause to go through embarrassing or nervous moments. It's all cut and dried, and whether you get the loan or not depends solely on how your credit rating stacks up. Other kinds of loans are treated with the same coolness and lack of pressure on you. All that's to your advantage.

On the other hand, the computer is programmed to say yes to your loan request only if you meet high standards of credit-worthiness which not all of us can meet. And that's a *big* disadvantage.

So weighing advantages over disadvantages, I would say this: A commercial bank is a fine place to go for a loan provided your credit rating is unblemished.

• *Evaluating savings banks.*   Interest rates are the same as commercial banks' right across the board, except that rates on passbook loans may be somewhat less. Times to pay tend overall to be shorter than those offered by commercial banks: up to three years for personal loans as contrasted with five years in commercial banks, and up to one year for passbook loans as opposed to three to five. Even mortgage payments tend to be shorter: twenty-five years tops; it's thirty-five years in commercial banks. On second mortgages and home improvement loans, length of payment is about the same as that of commercial banks.

What do all those numbers mean? Just this—that on the whole, you'll have less time to pay off your loans, which in turn means that each of your payments will be larger than if you were dealing with a commercial bank. That could be a big disadvantage if you're planning to use most of your income for other than debt-repayment purposes. On the other hand, the longer your debt payments the more interest you pay, so shorter term loans save you money. That's an advantage.

"What's better, Dr. Meltzer—a long-term loan with easy payments, or a short-term loan which will save me money?" is a question which occurs over and over again. Consumer advocates will answer, "The short-term loan without any question." And that's one reason they have a bias toward savings banks in preference to commercial banks for consumer loans. But you have to look at the problem in terms of your life situation. If you can afford to pay back the loan fast without any strain on the way you live, of course a short-term loan is better. But if you can't—if small loan payments mean you and your family can use the remainder of your income to enjoy some of the good things of life—then a long-term loan is better for you.

Meltzerism:
A long-term loan doesn't always mean you're selling yourself short.

It's easier to get a mortgage at a savings bank than at a commercial bank, but it's harder to get a second mortgage. So far as other kinds of loans are concerned, they're treated with the same objectivity as at a commercial bank—and you can get any kind of loan at a savings bank that you can get at a commercial bank.

The savings bank ordinarily doesn't have the slick, efficient atmosphere of a commercial bank, and as a general customer you're not offered the same range of services, but looking at the bank strictly as a source of loans, you can do as well at a savings bank as at a commercial bank if you're willing to pay up faster.

• *Evaluating savings and loan associations.* Interest rates are the same as those of savings banks. The facilities for mortgage loans are probably better here than at any other kind of bank. Repayment times are the same as those of savings banks. Savings and loan associations compare favorably with savings banks.

• *Evaluating credit unions.* The big advantage here is that interest rates are at least ¼ percent lower than at commercial banks. Another advantage is that if you're a member of a credit union, it is almost impossible to be turned down for a loan. Overall payment times are longer than at a commercial bank. Two examples: twelve years on a signature loan, as compared to three at a commercial bank; fifteen years on a home improvement loan, as compared to ten—and that's a benefit to you, since you'll be repaying with consistently shrinking dollars. The atmosphere is far warmer and friendlier than at other banks because you're dealing with people you know. The popularity of credit unions is enormous; there are now more than 35 million members nationwide. Deservedly so, because as a consumer loan source it is, in every way, preferable to the commercial bank and the other two kinds of bank. The big drawback is, you have to be a member to use the services of a credit union.

• *Evaluating second mortgage companies.* Interest rates are boosted by "charges," so overall figure you're paying at least 3 percent more than at a commercial bank. Repayment time is the same as that of a commercial bank. There are two big advantages in dealing with these firms, though: Second mortgages are easier to get than at any bank; and you can get small second mortgages which commercial banks, particularly, will not accept. Second mortgage companies are the places to go to when your requests for second mortgages have been turned down elsewhere.

One question that comes up now and then is: "I have equity on my home of $20,000. I have a first mortgage and a second mortgage. Can I still raise money on my equity?" Yes, you can. You can get a third mortgage. And, if you still have equity, you can get a fourth mortgage, and so on. When you're looking for third and fourth mortgages, go to the second mortgage companies—the going's easier there. And that's another advantage they have over banks.

• *Evaluating security brokers.* This is a very specialized place to go to raise money. Not all brokers advance cash, and you must have a sizable portfolio before the broker will say yes. You must be a preferred customer—and, of course, you must be the kind of person who plays the securities game. Borrowing here is also very expensive—about 2 or 3 points over prime rate.

"What's prime rate?" is a frequent question. That's the rate banks charge to their preferred business customers. When you take a loan at any bank you're not directly influenced by the prime rate because consumer loan rates are fixed by state laws. That works out as a good thing for you, because prime rates have in the past been higher than consumer loan rates—and they undoubtedly will be higher in the future. You can be sure of one thing, though: When prime rates go up, the banks will make every effort to raise the rates on consumer loans.

To get back to the security brokers. Assuming that the prime rate is just 1 percentage point over the consumer loan rate at a commercial bank, then you'll be paying 3 to 4 percentage points more for your money from a broker than you would from a commercial bank. Actually, you could put up your securities at a commercial bank, get up to 75 percent of their value (not just up to 50 percent, which is all that is offered by brokers), and save on interest costs. Then why do some people get the money from their brokers? For one thing, it's easy—just a phone call and no red tape.

Here's another drawback of dealing with a broker. Let's say you have a portfolio worth $100,000. You borrow up to your limit—$50,000. But the market takes a dive. Your portfolio is worth only $80,000. Now, 50 percent of $80,000 is $40,000. But the broker has given you $50,000—$10,000 too much. So he gives you a choice: "Put up $10,000 or I'll sell $10,000 worth of your securities." Not a happy situation.

All in all, I think borrowing from a broker is a financially unhealthy situation.

• *Evaluating credit card companies.* Interest rates and length of repayment (up to three years) are the same as those of bank cards. The credit card, whether bank or T&E, remains the easiest way to get cash when you need it.

• *Evaluating life insurance companies.* Interest rates are extremely low for personal loans, ranging from 4 percent (if you bought the policy some time ago) to 8 percent (if you bought it recently)—and that's from 13 to 17 percent lower than commercial policy maximums. Usually, the interest is added onto your premiums, but—and here's the unusual thing about this kind of loan—you can pay it back whenever you like in any amounts that suit you. That makes repayment easy on you. But that has its drawback: The amount you don't pay back (and you don't have to pay anything back if you don't want to) plus interest is subtracted from the amount paid to your beneficiary. That may well be something you don't want to happen.

A life insurance loan is easy to get—just make a written request to the insurance company. Add that to the other advantages and you can see why borrowing on life insurance policies has become increasingly popular.

There's another very interesting way you can raise money on your insurance policy, and the best way for me to tell you about it is as follows: A man phones in and says, "I need cash, Dr. Meltzer, and I'm told by several of my friends that I should cash in my whole life policy and take out a term policy. What shall I do?" I say, "How old are you?" And he says, "Sixty." I say, "How old is the policy?" He says,

"Twenty-two years." I say, "What's its cash surrender value?" That's the amount of money he'll get if he cashes in on the policy; it's often less than the cash value on which he can make a loan. He says, "$35,000." I say, "Are you in good health? Do you think you can pass an insurance doctor's exam?" He says, "Absolutely." "Do it," I say. And I tell him why:

At this stage of his life, he doesn't need to use an insurance policy as a savings device; he's educated his kids, they've flown the nest. So drawing out the $35,000 is okay. But he still wants insurance for his widow. So he buys term for five years (he can always renew it) at about half the cost of his whole life. Now he has $35,000 in cash and he's saving about $500 a year. He's way ahead. And I tell him, "You could be even further ahead if you invested the money in CDs paying about 15 percent. At the end of the year, the money you had locked up in your policy could be earning about $5,000 more for you." He says, "Dr. Meltzer, that's why I needed the cash in the first place."

• *Evaluating small loan companies.* As I've already told you, small loan companies are good places to go to get small loans which banks find unprofitable to make. They're also places to go to get personal loans, auto loans, and second mortgages when banks say no. Credit standards are much lower than at commercial banks; and very often the fact that you're working at some job for a year or more is enough to qualify you. People don't exude friendliness, and there's not that slick atmosphere you get in most banks, but you do get the loan—and that's what counts. You get the same time to pay as you'd get at a commercial bank, and that's fine too. But—and here's the hitch—you end up paying up to three times the interest you would pay on a personal loan at a commercial bank, and about twice what you would pay on an auto loan, and a good 4 or 5 percentage points more than you would pay on a second mortgage.

I want to repeat that when you can't get these three kinds of loans elsewhere, and you need them, *really* need them, you should go to a personal loan company. But remember, you're paying more because for you it's the only wheel in town.

• *Evaluating industrial loan companies.* Just imagine a personal loan company with rates slashed in half. That's an industrial loan company. They're not everywhere, so look in your Yellow Pages. If it's a choice between dealing with an industrial loan company and a personal finance company, take the industrial loan.

• *Evaluating your employer.* I've already done that for you so far as the psychological aspects are concerned. Interest rates tend to be somewhat lower than those of commercial banks, and are about on a par with those at credit unions. But there's no standard, and a talk with the loan officer at your company's loan department (if it has one) should give you all the facts about costs and repayment times as well. Turndowns are rare, and people are friendly.

• *Evaluating executive loan services.*   Rates are about 6 percentage points higher than those at commercial banks, and repayment time is about the same. Big advantage is that you can transact the whole business by mail in many cases, or in friendly face-to-face sessions in others. To get the picture of an executive loan service, look at it as a personal loan company for people making good money at good jobs. It can be useful when you need a large wad of money fast, and your credit line is exhausted everyplace else. But expect rates to be higher than those of commercial banks.

• *Evaluating pawnshops.*   I once saw a limo pull up in front of a pawnshop, and a fashionably dressed woman get out carrying her fur coat on her arm. Why not?—it was spring, and she wouldn't need it again for several months, and in the meantime she could use some spare cash. The pawnshop was one of the reputable ones—it looked more like a bank than the seedy pawnshops you see in the movies. At a reputable pawnshop you get up to a year to redeem your pledge, and you can lower the amount of interest on the loan by making partial payments during the year. Interest rates are no higher than what a bank would charge. If you forfeit your pledge by nonpayment, it's sold at public auction; and if it brings in more than what you owe on it, *you*—not the pawnshop—get the surplus. Most reputable pawnshops limit their loans to pledges of gold, silver, furs, gems, stamps, and coins.

If you have anything else to pawn, then you have to go to the shoddy pawnshops. *They* look like the kind you see in the movies. At these pawnshops, rates are at least 6 percentage points higher than at commercial banks, and often you only have a month to redeem your pledge. If you can't raise the money in that time, you'll lose a possession worth at least four times what you pawned it for. The people at these pawnshops are not noted for their charm, and often you'll be treated crudely. They expect you to bargain, but be warned: These pawnbrokers are among the shrewdest bargainers you'll ever meet.

The advantages of dealing with a pawnshop of any kind are, as I've already told you, twofold. One, you get on-the-spot cash. And two, you can raise money on an item you have no use for for a short period of time.

One last word about pawnshops. If you find you can't redeem an item, you can *sell* your pawn ticket to another pawnbroker and receive up to 25 percent of the money you raised.

BERNARD MELTZER'S ADVICE
ON THE BEST PLACES TO BORROW

Banks are your best bets. The credit union is the best bank source; loans are the cheapest there and easiest to get. Use other loan sources only when the banks say no.

ARE INTEREST RATES THE ONLY COSTS OF BORROWING?

No. There are other fees which can be included. These vary from lender to lender, so when you take out a loan it's best to find out what your total "finance charge" will be. But that's not all you have to worry about when you borrow. Interest can be calculated in three basically different ways, and the way it's calculated can greatly affect your total charge. The arithmetic is complicated, and we don't have to go into it, but the "add-on" method of interest calculations costs you less than the "discount" method. So if you shop around, say, to Bank A and Bank B, and they offer you the same interest rates, but Bank A tells you it calculates interest by the add-on method and Bank B tells you it calculates interest by the discount method, buy at Bank A if you're out to save money. The third way is the "rule of 78." If you can possibly avoid it, do so; it's the most harmful way of calculating interest ever to be forced on the consumer.

Chapter 5

How to Get Your Loan Approved

When I was growing up, borrowing was regarded as shameful. Poor as we were, we never borrowed. But strangely enough, some of the virtues I was taught as a boy by my parents now make it possible for me to get any kind of loan should I desire it. What are those virtues? Honesty, to begin with. And a sense of responsibility. Trustworthiness. Plus a knowledge of right and wrong. And stability and good sound common sense. Why are those virtues esteemed by a lender? Because a person who practices these virtues will never borrow over his head, and he will pay back every cent on or before the time it is due. A person with these virtues, a lender says, has *character*. When a lender recognizes that you have character, you're on your way to getting a loan.

But character must be backed up by your ability to repay. And to have that ability for most of us who weren't born with silver spoons in our mouths means the willingness to work, to stay with a job, to get ahead. On the scoreboard, those virtues take the form of an income large enough to support you and your family comfortably while you repay the loan. The lender calls your income and the virtues that produced it your *capacity* to repay. That capacity plus character means you can get the loan.

Put all the virtues behind character and capacity together and back them up with faith in yourself and the will to win, and in America, as in no other place in the world, you can pile up *capital*. That doesn't only mean money in the bank; it also means any asset of considerable value —your securities, for example, or your home. With sufficient capital you need not have capacity. Capital and character can get you the loan.

What lenders of any type look for are character, capacity, and capital —the three C's of credit.

Credit applications usually are means to discover whether you possess the three C's. Let's look at a typical application and discover the best way to fill it out to get approval of your loan.

16. HOW TO KNOW IF YOU'LL GET A LOAN.

The form on the following page is a reproduction of one used by a leading national commercial bank for a personal loan, auto loan, or home improvement loan. I've added the numbers to indicate those lines which are important to the loan officer (and the computer) in judging whether you have the C's necessary for an okay. Now I'd like to discuss the numbers and what the lines they stand for mean. Before you read my interpretation of the lines, please fill in each line as if you were applying for a loan. I want to warn you that this is going to be pretty detailed. But it will pay off. So—

Line 1: Marital status. Although line 1 is optional (sex discrimination is frowned on by the statute makers), if you are a Mrs., it's wise to check the box. The reason is as follows: The banker is looking for a sense of responsibility, and in his or her eyes, a married person is more responsible than a single one. Responsibility indicates *character*. So a Mrs. gets you a check next to line 1.

Line 2: Age. If you're under sixty-two, you have the *capacity* to earn enough to repay a three-year loan. Over sixty-two, you have less than three years to retirement, and your income may be so severely cut at retirement that you may not be able to make payments. After sixty-five, the usual retirement age, you're a poor risk for a loan. You get a check next to line 2 when you're under sixty-two.

Line 3: Neighborhood. The assumption is if you live in a good neighborhood, you have the *capacity* to pay. This is not always a wise assumption. Rentals on the Upper East Side of Manhattan are so expensive that there's little left over for anything else. And I know of several young couples who have bought houses in good neighborhoods and are paying so much on their mortgage each month that they have no money for furniture. But banks do put a heavy reliance on neighborhoods. So do other credit sources. Several years ago three major department stores in Manhattan offered charge plates by phone to people in better sections of town; all the prospect had to do to get the plates was say, "Yes, send them." No application or credit check was required. If you live in a good neighborhood you get a check next to line 3.

Lines 4–5: Your residence. If you've been at the same residence for

Credit Application
Check All Applicable Boxes)

☐ I apply for an instalment loan of $_____ for _____ months.

Loan Purpose _____
Number of Days to First Payment ☐ 30 ☐ 45 ☐ 60
☐ Deduct Monthly Instalment Loan Payments from my Checking Account.

☐ I Apply for a Cash Reserve of $_____ Joint Account with _____
☐ I apply for a Cash Reserve increase to $_____
Joint Account with _____

Credit Insurance is optional. It is not a condition to approval of your application. If you think you want insurance, please check the applicable box below.
☐ Credit Life and Disability Insurance
☐ Credit Life Insurance only
If you check a box, we will prepare your loan accordingly. However, you will still be free to take the loan without the insurance.

☐ I Apply for a Visa Account
Checking Account No. _____
Send Mail to ☐ Home ☐ Office

NO. _____

CAR PURCHASE INFORMATION		
Year	Make	Price $
Seller		Down payment $
To be registered in the name of		SerialNo. if known

TELL US ABOUT YOURSELF (APPLICANT) PLEASE PRINT AND COMPLETE ALL INFORMATION

1 ☐ MR. ☐ MS ☐ MRS. ☐ MISS *(Optional)* — LAST NAME / FIRST NAME / INITIAL / SOCIAL SECURITY NO.

HOME ADDRESS — NUMBER AND STREET / APARTMENT / NO. DEPENDENTS **5** / ☐ OWN HOME ☐ RENT ☐ MO. PYMT. $

3 CITY AND STATE / ZIP CODE / HOW LONG YRS. MO. **4** / AREA CODE HOME TEL. NO.

6 PREVIOUS HOME ADDRESS — NUMBER AND STREET / CITY AND STATE / ZIP CODE / HOW LONG YRS. MO. / DATE OF BIRTH MONTH DAY YEAR **2**

7 NAME OF BUSINESS OR EMPLOYER / MO. SALARY $ / HOW LONG YRS. MO. / BUS. TEL. NO. EXT.

BUSINESS ADDRESS / CITY AND STATE / ZIP CODE / TYPE OF BUSINESS / POSITION **8**

9 You need not disclose alimony, child support, separate maintenance income or its source, unless you want us to consider it in connection with this application. / OTHER INCOME AND SOURCE OF OTHER INCOME $

10 NAME OF PREVIOUS BUSINESS OR EMPLOYER / BUSINESS ADDRESS **11** / HOW LONG YRS. MO.

PERSONAL REFERENCE

12 NAME OF RELATIVE NOT LIVING WITH YOU / ADDRESS / RELATIONSHIP / TELEPHONE NO.

CREDIT REFERENCES

13 CHECKING ACCOUNT (Bank Name, Branch and Address) / ☐ PERSONAL ☐ BUSINESS / ☐ OVERDRAFT CHECKING LINE OF CREDIT **14** / ACCOUNT NUMBER

15 SAVINGS ACCOUNT (Bank Name, Branch and Address) / BALANCE $ / ACCOUNT NUMBER

16 HOME FINANCED BY / ORIGINAL MTG. AMT. $ / PRESENT BAL. $ / EST. VALUE $ / RENTAL INCOME $ **17**

Please list all loans, credit lines and credit cards. If a joint account, list for both applicants (Attach separate sheet if necessary)

	CREDITOR AND ADDRESS	APPLICANT'S NAME	ACCOUNT NO.	ORIGINAL AMT.	BALANCE	MO. PAY.
18 LOANS						
19 CREDIT LINES & CARDS						

20 DO YOU OWN A CAR? ☐ YES ☐ NO / YEAR AND MAKE / AMOUNT OWING / CREDITOR

21 CO-APPLICANT
Provide the following information only if you are relying on another person's income for credit or if another person is applying with you for a joint account (either referred to below as "co-applicant")

Please check the applicable boxes)
☐ Co-applicant is applying with you for a joint account
☐ Co-applicant is someone on whose income you are relying for credit
Relationship of Co-applicant ☐ Spouse ☐ Other

CO-APPLICANT'S LAST NAME / FIRST NAME / INITIAL / SOCIAL SECURITY NUMBER

HOME ADDRESS / CITY AND STATE / ZIP CODE / HOME TELEPHONE NO. / DATE OF BIRTH MONTH DAY YR.

CO-APPLICANT'S BUSINESS OR EMPLOYER / MONTHLY SALARY $ / POSITION

BUSINESS ADDRESS / HOW LONG YEARS MO.

CITY AND STATE / ZIP CODE / BUSN. TELEPHONE & EXT.

You need not disclose alimony, child support, separate maintenance income or its source, unless you want us to consider it in connection with this application. / OTHER INCOME AND SOURCE OF OTHER INCOME $

IMPORTANT NOTICE ABOUT CREDIT REPORTS

A consumer credit report or reports may be requested from one or more consumer reporting agencies (credit bureaus) in connection with this application. Subsequent consumer credit reports may be requested or used in connection with any update, renewal or extension of the credit requested by this application. If you request, you will be informed whether any consumer credit report was requested and, if so, of the name and address of the consumer reporting agency or agencies which furnished the report.

AGREEMENT

1. **Application** — By signing below as applicant or co-applicant for a joint account, I request the credit that I checked above.
2. **Credit Information** — I certify that the information above about me is true and complete. I authorize you, or sources to which you may apply or which may apply to you, to exchange credit information about me with respect to this application or any indebtedness to you or any account which you open as a result of this application. I also agree that you may obtain and use the consumer credit reports described above.
3. **Visa Card Applicants** — If I am applying for a Visa card, I agree that use of the Visa card by me, or by anyone I authorize, will be my acceptance of the credit agreement which accompanies the Visa card which you issue to me.

PLEASE SIGN HERE

APPLICANT AND CO-APPLICANT IF ANY ▶ APPLICANT'S SIGNATURE / CO-APPLICANT'S SIGNATURE / DATE

ICD597(L) Rev. 7-79

1 2 3 4 5 6 7 8 9 / CU/RSN / DATE / A R / SOURCE / BRANCH NO. / DATE OPENED / AVG. BALANCE

more than five years that's a sign of a solid citizen, so for *character* you get a check next to line 4. If you own your own home, you're regarded as a more solid citizen than if you rent; so for *character*, you get another check beside line 4. And if you pay rent or mortgage payments in excess of $500 a month, it's assumed you have the capacity to pay a loan, and you get another check.

Line 5: Dependents. Having dependents is another sign of stability. So if you have dependents you get a check next to line 5 as a tribute to your *character*. But if you have more than four dependents, your capacity to pay comes into question, and although you will get a check for *character*, you may get an X for *capacity*, which cancels out the check.

Line 6: Length of time at previous residence. A stay of at least five years at your previous residence is another sign of your stability; so for *character*, you get another check next to line 6.

Line 7: Income from, and length of time on, the job. If you earn more than $15,000 a year, and you've been on the job for more than one year, that shows *capacity*, which earns you a check next to line 7.

Line 8: Your business and job title. If you're in a business that's been around for some time and is likely to be around for some time, that means you have the *capacity* to pay, and it earns you a check on this line. You won't get it if you're working for, say, a mom-and-pop store. You earn another check if you're a blue-collar worker or member of management (even if you're a foreman), since you have the *capacity* to pay. But you'll get no check if you're a clerical worker, because turnover is too rapid, and you may not have the *capacity* to pay.

A question I frequently hear is: "I'm self-employed. Do I have a chance of getting a loan?" I say, "What are you employed at?" And if they say, "I'm an actor," or "I'm an artist," or "I'm a free-lance writer," I say, "You have next to no chance. The only chance you have is to get out your WC-2 forms for the past several years, or get out your income tax forms, or get out your royalty statements, and show them to the bank to prove your *capacity* to pay. Otherwise the bank will assume no *capacity,* and you'll get a big X next to line 8. One big X can knock out your loan request."

On the other hand, if you're a self-employed lawyer, accountant, dentist, or doctor, you'll get a check next to line 8. The assumption is you'll have the *capacity* to pay.

Line 9: Income from other sources. Any steady income over $5,000 a year increases your *capacity* to pay, and gets you a check. If the income comes from your assets, such as stocks or bonds, you also earn a check for *capital.*

Lines 10–11: Your previous job. The bank would like to know that over the last five to six years, you had a good job with a stable firm, on the theory that future performances can be predicted from past performances. In other words, if you had the *capacity* to pay for five to six years, you'll have the *capacity* to pay for the duration of the loan. You only fill out this line if you haven't been on your present job for more than 3 years; so 2 to 3 years on a previous good job should entitle you to a check against these lines.

Line 12: Name of a relative. Any verifiable name gets you a check. All the bank wants to know is who to call in case you and your spouse skip town.

Lines 13–15: Your deposit accounts. Checking and savings accounts represent *capital.* If your combined balance exceeds $3,000, you'll get a check for this line. You'll get additional checks for a combined balance over $10,000, and for accounts in the bank at which you're requesting a loan. These days, it's downright silly to keep more than the amount of money you need to cover six months' expenses in a savings or checking account. You can get about three times the interest in a CD. If you have CDs, put down the information on a separate sheet of paper, and attach. That will earn you a check; and if the CDs are with the bank at which you're requesting a loan, you'll get another check.

An overdraft checking line of credit means that you have been previously cleared for a loan, and that earns you a big check because you've met the requirements of all three C's.

Lines 16–17: Your home. Getting a mortgage means you're an established 3-C person. That earns a big check. Add a check if your equity in your home is above $25,000. (You can figure the equity by subtracting mortgage balance from estimated value.) Bankers like to know that you have sufficient *capital* you can turn into cash (in this case by a second mortgage or a refinancing of the first mortgage) in case things go wrong. An appreciable rental income will also earn you a check for *capacity.*

Lines 18–19: Your loans and credit cards. Having loans and credit cards also establishes you as a 3-C person, and that merits a big check. If you have had previous lines which you've paid in full, it's a good idea to enter them, and above the word *Balance* write 0. It's worth another check for each paid-off loan. Balances on loans and credit card balances helps the bank establish just how much you can borrow. I'll tell you about that shortly.

Line 20: A car is *capital,* and a car with substantial resale value is better capital than a ten-year-old jalopy. If you have this or last year's model of a medium- or high-priced car, you deserve a check.

Line 21: A co-applicant boosts your capacity to pay, so if you're not doing this on your own, you deserve a check next to this line, provided your co-applicant fills in information which would merit checks on the basis we've already discussed.

So, you see, a simple application form that you can fill out in a few minutes is really a complex thing. I hope you've been putting checks and X's against each line of the application form you've filled out. Because now I'm going to tell you what they mean to you as an applicant for a loan.

• *You'll get the loan provided* the amount you ask for is acceptable and you've passed a credit check. . . .

. . . *if* you have one or more big checks (for an overdraft checking line, a mortgage, or previous loans, lines 13–15, 16–17, and 18–19 respectively) plus checks on your income, business and job title, and deposit accounts lines (lines 7, 8, and 9 respectively)

. . . *if* you have no big checks, but in addition to checks on the income, business and job title, and deposit accounts lines, you have another ten checks

. . . *if* you have one big X (because you're self-employed in fields unacceptable to bankers) but also have at least one big check and another fifteen checks.

17. How to determine how much a bank will lend you.

The bank assumes you can handle a debt load of 10 percent of your gross monthly income (that's your income before deductions). If you have no outstanding debts, you can borrow up to the full 10 percent. For example, if your monthly salary is $1,000 you can borrow up to $100 a month provided you have no other debts. On a three-year loan that would amount to a total of $3,600—the most the bank would let you have. But suppose your debt load—from previous loans or credit card transactions, for example (lines 18–19 of your application)—amounts to $75 a month; then you can only get a loan repayable at $25 a month ($100 less $75), which amounts to only $900 for three years. And no bank will give you a loan for less than $3,000.

Here's a formula to use to determine your maximum loan:

• Take 10 percent of your gross monthly income
   (10 percent of $5,000 = $500)

- Subtract all your monthly loan and
  credit card payments
  ($500 − $300 = $200)
- Multiply by 36 (for a three-year loan)
  ($200 × 36 = $7,200)

18. ALL ABOUT CREDIT REPORTS.

Don't think just because you've filled out an application that a bank will approve, and don't think that because the amount of money you asked for is acceptable to the bank, you'll get it. You still have to pass a final test—the credit report. The bank (and for that matter any kind of firm you ask for credit) wants to know two things—one, if you are telling the truth on your application form; and two, if there is anything that they should know about you that can be held against you or considered in your favor. To learn this the bank hires a credit report bureau. Credit reports are so necessary to consumer finance that there are now some 2,500 credit report bureaus in the U.S.A. issuing about 150 million reports a year. Computers link almost all the bureaus in a national network of information about almost every adult in this country who has ever requested credit. If you have a bad credit record here, and you think by skipping to Florida you can start over again, put that thought out of your mind. Your record will be waiting for you there. But credit reports are a two-edged sword; if your credit record is good in your home town, you can get credit anywhere in the fifty states.

What's in a credit report? *Your true name and address,* for one thing. You'd be amazed how many people try to get credit under false names and addresses. *Your job.* Everybody knows that an "assistant manager in charge of shipping" has a better chance at a loan than a "stockroom boy." Your credit report may tell the bank you're really a stockroom boy. The report will also give *a true accounting of your present and your former earnings.* Many people exaggerate them. The report will state *how long you stayed at your residences.* Some people who know that bankers like you to live at one place for at least five years fill out loan applications that way even though they've just moved in. The report gives the banker the true facts. In short, what the report does, in part, is to tell the banker whether you were filling out the loan application truthfully or whether you puffed up the facts.

> **Meltzerism:**
> *Don't try to balloon your income or anything else to bankers. Credit report bureaus will bust the balloon every time.*

What else is in a credit report? Everything that's public about your financial life—that means every recorded financial transaction you made —*used to be* included on your credit report. But the government realized that wasn't fair. Let's say that twenty years ago you defaulted on a loan, but ever since you've been the soul of trustworthiness. Why should you be permanently penalized for that one slip in the past? So now the credit report can only cover your history for the past seven years. Bankers consider those seven years important on the theory that what you did in recent years you're most likely to do in the near future, which to my mind is pretty sound. So the report spells out how you handled your debt obligations over the last seven years. Did you pay on time? Did they have to send you lawyer's letters? Did they have to take you to court? And so on.

• *What credit report code numbers mean.* Most writers on credit will tell you that a credit report does not rate you as a good or bad risk; that the rating is actually done by the bank or other credit source. Strictly speaking, that's true. But when you look at a credit report you'll see a list of your creditors—Chase Visa, National Hanover MasterCharge, American Express, Texaco, Gump's, Bloomingdale's, and so on—and next to the name of each creditor, there will be a number from 0 to 9. Here's what the numbers mean:

0—Card approved but not yet used; too new for rating.

1—Pays account as agreed within thirty days of billing.

2—Slow pay. Pays in more than thirty days, but pays within sixty; is always one payment overdue.

3—Very slow pay. Pays in more than sixty days, but pays within ninety; is always two payments overdue.

4—Extremely slow pay. Pays in more than ninety days, but pays within 120 days; is always three payments overdue.

5—Non-pay. Is more than 120 days overdue.

6—This code number had a meaning once, but doesn't anymore, so it is not used.

7—Making partial payments under voluntary repayment arrangement, or has filed for Chapter 13 of the Bankruptcy Law, or is paying in accordance with Chapter 13.

8—Purchases repossessed because of inability to pay. But this is a tricky number; it also means purchases returned voluntarily—say, because they were faulty, or they didn't fit, or for whatever valid reason. When this is the case, the number 8 is usually followed by an explanation.

9—Bad debt. This means the bank or other credit source has handed over the account to a collection agency or its own legal department, or has given up hope of ever recovering even a part of the credit extended.

Now, you tell me if this coding system isn't really a rating system. If your credit report is a long list of 1's, that's like all A's in your school days. Your banker is very likely to say yes (provided you've met his other qualifications). If your report shows up a string of 2's and 3's, that's like all B's and C's, and you have a fair chance. But a single 4—like a D—makes the banker wary. And a single 5, 7, 8 (if repossession was due to nonpayment), or 9 is an F, and only under the most unusual circumstances will you get a loan. A 0 is as bad as an F. It means you haven't been tested yet, and a banker won't bet on you.

19. THE THREE QUALIFICATIONS FOR GETTING A LOAN.

You know them, because we've just gone through them. Simply to summarize:

The first qualification is: Fill out the application form honestly and to the satisfaction of the bank.

The second qualification is: Don't ask for more money than the bank feels you should get.

And the third qualification is: Be sure your credit report is coded 1.

20. HOW TO GET A GOOD CREDIT REPORT.

When you're starting out in life, very often you won't be able to get a loan or a credit card. A twenty-one-year-old woman comes to me and says, "I just got my master's degree in English literature, then my father sent me to Europe for two years to study French, and now I have a job with a publishing house here, but I can't get a credit card." I say, "Why do you want a credit card?" She says, "Well, when I travel, the clerks at the hotels just won't register me unless I have a credit card." I say, "Why don't you tell them you'll pay cash in advance?" She says, "Some of them won't accept cash. They say it fouls up the computer. Others say, 'Go see the credit manager,' and that's a long-drawn-out business, and the credit managers are not very nice if you don't have a credit card." She goes on to say, "Dr. Meltzer, did you ever try to rent a car without a credit card?" I never did, but I know that it's almost impossible. I say, "So your problem is—how do you get a credit card?" "Yes," she says, "I wish you could tell me how."

I tell this story because credit cards are easy to get, and once you get one, and do as I tell you with it, you can get others, and you can get loans. The first thing to do is open up both checking and savings accounts at the same bank at which later on you'll apply for a loan. At the end of your first year on the job—not before—do two things: First, boost your combined total on your accounts to over $3,000. If you have to borrow temporarily from a friend or a loving member of your family, do it. Second, fill out a credit card application. Few starting jobs these days pay less than $10,000 a year, unless it's for unskilled labor; and if you make $10,000 a year or more, and have been in the same job for a year, and have accounts worth more than $3,000 at the bank, you'll get a card—even though your credit report shows an absolute blank regarding your credit history. Your credit line will be minimum, $500, but you *have* a card—and now you can go about establishing a good credit rating with it.

Use your card. "But Dr. Meltzer," I've had people say to me, "consumer advocates say that using a credit card can get you into trouble." There's no way it can get you into trouble if you're a safe borrower, no way at all. As a matter of fact, it's silly not to use your card, as you'll find out later on in this book.

To get back to getting a good credit report. Use your credit card, and pay back before the agreed due date every month, month in and month out for nine months to a year. Never exceed your credit line limit. Now you have a credit record that ranks 1. Now go to two other banks and apply for credit cards. "Wait a minute," somebody always says to me when I reach this point, "you say get *two* more credit cards?" I say, "Yes." And whoever's talking to me says, "But there are only two bank credit cards, Visa and MasterCharge. How can you get *three* cards?" The answer is there are as many different Visa cards as there are banks issuing them, and the same is true of MasterCharge cards. So you can have Bank A's Visa, and Bank B's Visa, and Bank C's Visa, and on and on. And you can have Bank A's MasterCharge, and Bank B's MasterCharge, and Bank C's MasterCharge, and so forth. It's possible to obtain credit cards from every bank in town; and there are some credit card "freaks" who actually do it—you read about them now and then; there's actually a nut with a thousand or more credit cards from all sources. But I'd think three more or less is a sensible number.

Now you have three credit cards. What you do is, use them, and run up a perfect repayment record for six months minimum. And now's the time to apply for a loan, even though you don't need it. That's because you're going to use the loan to continue to build up your credit report. On the basis of your credit report—1,1,1—and your job and your deposits at the bank, you'll get a modest loan—say, $3,000. Take it out for three years, but pay it back in one. Now you have four 1's on your credit report.

From now on it should be easy to add 1's. Apply for charge accounts at major department stores. You'll get them. Then use them for the things you need, and pay back before due dates. Get other "single-purpose" cards as well—cards from oil companies, hotel chains, restaurants, airlines, and so forth. Use them when you need them, repay before due dates, and your credit report will soon read 1, 1, 1, 1, 1, 1, 1, 1, 1, 1, 1, 1 . . . Now you'll have a perfect credit report; and when you really need a loan, you'll be able to get it without any trouble.

"Is it worth all this fuss," I'm asked, "just to set up a good credit record? I may never need a loan." True enough, but it's unlikely that you'll go through life without asking for credit at one time or another. You'll want to buy a car, won't you? Or a house? Or a boat? Or a piece of property? When you get right down to it . . . but let me say it in the form of a—

Meltzerism:
These days it's as important to have a good credit report as it is to have a good job.

21. THE COST OF GETTING A GOOD CREDIT REPORT.

"To get a good credit report, aren't you spending more money than you have to?" is a question I usually get thrown at me. The answer is no. For one thing, you only buy what you need—things you would have bought anyway. And if you pay *before* due date—remember, I recommended that you do just that—there is no finance charge on credit charge or charge plate accounts. And the answer is also yes—there's nothing black and white in this life—because bank cards cost $15 a year, and you have to pay interest on your loan at between 18 and 21 percent, so on a $3,000 loan you'll be out about $600 if you pay it back in a year. But if you put that $3,000 in a CD earning about 11 percent you'll get back more than half of that $600. Your cost—with three bank cards and the loan—will come to around $350. That's cheap for what you're getting.

22. HOW TO MAKE MONEY WHILE GETTING A GOOD CREDIT REPORT.

Instead of taking out a signature loan, take out a passbook loan. As you know, while you're paying up to 12 percent on your loan, you're earning 5¼ percent on your savings, so the loan doesn't cost you 12 percent, but only 6¾ percent. (By contrast, a signature loan costs you up to 22.5 percent, and only comes down to 10 percent when you invest the money in a CD.) Now invest the 6¾ percent money in a CD at 11 percent, and you're actually making 4¼ percent on your loan!

Because a passbook loan is cheaper than a signature loan, many people start building a good credit report with a passbook loan, even when they don't invest the money in a CD. But a passbook loan has a small drawback so far as your credit standing is concerned. It's a *secured* loan, and it does not provide a history of repayment on an *unsecured* loan. So when you apply for an unsecured loan, the loan officer might say to himself, "This person has never paid back an unsecured loan before—how do I know he'll do it when his property is not at stake?"— and even though you earned your 1, it may not mean anything. But that's only when fairly large sums of money are at stake. For modest loans, the 1 you earn on prompt repayment of a secured loan will count. It's *your* future—do you plan to make big personal loans or small ones? If you plan to make big ones, then it might be a good idea to prove right off the bat that you can pay off an unsecured loan faster than required—even though it will cost you some dollars to prove it.

23. HOW TO TURN A BAD CREDIT REPORT AROUND.

Sometimes the bad report is no fault of yours. Let me tell you a story:

My friend Andy Casey applied for a T&E card, and a few weeks later, he got a rejection notice in the mail. Now Andy is one of the most honest and trustworthy men I know. He is so scrupulous about paying off his debts that he actually circles each due date in red on his calendar, and hangs his calendar right over his desk. So when the rejection notice came in he was shocked. He called me up, and he said, "Bernie, what should I do?" Now I knew that Andy earned $75,000 a year, had his own home, had been working in top middle management for the same giant corporation for years, and had the complete profile for acceptance for credit anywhere, so I said, "The computer goofed." And he said, "What do I do about it?" I replied, "Look at your rejection notice." He said, "Wait a minute, I'll get it." He did and he said, "What now?" I said, "Look for the name of the credit bureau." He found it. And I said, "They made a mistake. What you have to do is write them a letter and ask them to send you a Xerox of the report they sent the credit card company." He asks, "Will they do it?" I said, "If they don't, they'll have Uncle Sam to reckon with. It's the law."

Andy followed my instructions, and in about two weeks he got a copy of the report. It was full of 9's. According to the report, Andy Casey of New Orleans was one of the greatest deadbeats of all time. But the Andy Casey I knew lived in Philadelphia. The credit card bureau had submitted a report on the wrong Andy Casey! It took my Andy Casey about three months to straighten things out—telephone calls and letters—but he finally did it, and he got his T&E card.

Unusual? Credit card bureaus admit they make mistakes in about 2 percent of the cases. That sounds small until you consider that 2 percent of 150 million reports a year is 3 million. The credit card bureaus admit to making 3 million mistakes a year! So what happened to Andy Casey could happen to you. But if it does, all you do is send the right information to the credit bureau—they'll check it out—and if they agree with you, they'll alter the report in your favor. Every loan rejection must by law carry the name and address of the credit bureau that supplied the credit report, so you'll know where to go to start the ball rolling.

For most of us, though, a bad credit report is not the credit bureau's fault; it's ours. We've become careless, and rolled up a lot of 2's, 3's, and 4's. Your credit report is not terrible, but it's far from good. You can turn it around by turning yourself around. From now on, on all your outstanding accounts, pay on time. In about six months, the 2's, 3's, and 4's will start turning to 1's. It's that simple.

But let's take the worst possible case: Your report comes back with a list of 9's. Those 9's are going to stay on your report for seven years, and there's nothing you can do about it. But after seven years, start fresh by building up a good credit report the way I've already described to you. I've known many bankrupts who have done it, and now are enjoying the use of credit just as most of us do.

24. CREDIT REPORTS AND PRIVACY.

Anybody can draw a credit report on you (and you can draw a credit report on anybody). Today many employers will do it when you apply for a job. You can understand the reason. They would like an employee who possesses all the three C's—*character, capacity,* and *capital.* That's the kind of man or woman an employer can depend on. When your credit report turns up no C's, your prospective employer is likely to turn you down. I think that's fair; dependability means productivity, and that's what an employer is looking for. It doesn't matter how smart you are or how well-educated or experienced, if you don't come to the job to *work* and give it your all, day in and day out, you're a poor employee, and your prospective employer should know it in advance. A lack of the three C's is a warning signal.

On the other hand, any snoop can get your credit report just by paying for it. If the guy in the next house wants to know what his new neighbor is like, all he has to do is buy a report from the nearest credit bureau. That means so far as your economic life is concerned, and so far as your character profile is concerned, you might just as well be living in a goldfish bowl. Fair? "Absolutely not," almost everybody I talk to says, and I agree. "But there's nothing we can do about it," they say, throwing up their hands. "Absolutely nothing."

Wrong. There *is* something you can do about it. Live your financial life so clean that when the snoops draw the report on you they'll find only the three C's and they'll come away with admiration, even if they find you're not making as much money as you'd like them to think you're making. People are impressed by a display of the good old-fashioned virtues, and they'll think more of you for having them. And you'll think more of yourself, too. You know, a lot of sophisticates these days sneer at those virtues—"Boy Scout virtues," they call them— but without such virtues you're not going to get a good credit report, and without a good credit report you're really a second-class citizen. With a good credit report, you can buy what you want within the limits of your income; you can even borrow to invest and get ahead in the world; and most of all, you can reassure yourself that you can become anything you want to become, because it's proof you have the character to do so. It might not be a bad idea if you did a little snooping on yourself, and sent to your nearest credit bureau (it's in the Yellow Pages) for your own credit report. If it's not what you think it should be, the sight of it will be a powerful incentive to you to become a better person and a more successful one.

25. The Personal Approach to Getting a Loan Approved.

A good friend of mine is worth several million dollars. He can walk into a bank—and I've seen him do this—and sit down in the president's office, and say, "Joe, I need a couple of hundred thousand dollars." Joe and my friend are buddies; they play golf together, they belong to the same country club, they socialize with the same kind of well-heeled people. "Sure," Joe says, "I'll get the paperwork going immediately." And there's nothing wrong with that. Joe knows my friend, knows he has all the three C's, knows that a credit report would be a long string of 1's, and, most of all, knows that my friend has borrowed from his bank many times before, and no matter how large the sums involved, always has paid them back on time.

But unless you're wealthy and know the bank president or a top executive on a person-to-person basis, you can't just walk into the bank and get a loan on your say-so. Granting a loan is for the most part an impersonal and computerized decision. But bank officers are human, and they can be influenced. I know of a young man who was just starting out with his own public relations business. He ran into a bad stretch and lost a few clients, and although he had enough money to keep his business going, he couldn't draw any salary for himself. He needed a loan, but his income was zero; he had fallen behind on his debt payments; so his credit report was full of 2's and 3's; and he only had a few dollars in his savings and checking accounts. He went to the loan officer of his bank, a VP, and said, "The furniture in my office is expensive, and it's almost new—with business the way it is these days, there's nobody there to wear it out—so I'd like to put it up as collateral for a personal loan." The loan officer told him the bank wouldn't accept that kind of collateral. But then he asked the young man why he needed the loan. The young man told him the whole story honestly, and added, "I have a few new accounts pending. I'm sure I'm going to land one or two of them, and then everything will be all right." The loan officer was impressed by the young man's sincerity, and said, "I don't think I'm taking a chance. I'm going to give you a personal loan, and you don't have to put up anything as security."

It can be done. Women, especially unmarried women, have an especially difficult job getting loans when they don't meet bank standards. It's against the law to discriminate against women, and it's morally wrong as well; but it is a fact of life. Yet one woman I know moved to Houston from the East, got herself a small apartment, got herself a job as a secretary with an airline, had her loan application turned down, went to the bank, spoke to the loan officer, and got the loan. She told me, "I simply told him I had spent most of my money making the move and getting settled in, I was in love with Houston and I migrated from the East so I could stay here all the rest of my life, and that there was a young man in my life and we intended to get married soon, and I needed the money for necessities like a new wardrobe suitable for Texas, and that I *could* pay back the monthly installments, and I was sincere as all blazes when I told him I would pay back every cent on time."

If you get a rejection, or if you feel your credit record doesn't justify a loan, you can go in and talk to the loan officer. If you decide to do so, here are—

• *Guidelines for influencing a loan officer.* Basically, you influence a bank officer the same way you influence anyone else—by putting your best foot forward.

Don't be intimidated just by being in a bank. Look at it this way: A bank is like any other kind of store. The only difference is, while other stores sell sofas and cigarettes and perfumes and so on, banks sell money. Think of them not as banks but as money stores; and think of the loan officer as like any guy or woman behind a counter—eager to sell you. The loan officer wants to find a way to say yes to your loan request, because that's the way his bank makes money. You're not intimidated when you do your shopping. What you're doing now is shopping for money. There's no reason in the world why you should feel uncomfortable. Be yourself.

Make a good appearance. Every section in the country has its own standard of what's acceptable daytime wear and what isn't. You don't have to dress up to go in for a loan; all you have to do is wear what's acceptable for a daytime business meeting in your neck of the woods. I'm an expert on at least thirteen fields of knowledge, but one field of knowledge I'm not an expert in is clothes, especially women's clothes. If you don't know what to wear at a meeting with your banker, do this the next time you go to the bank: Observe what the bank officers are wearing, then model your outfit on theirs. What you should never do is come in looking sloppy and unkempt.

Meltzerism:
An attractive appearance can help you attract a loan.

Tell your story simply and sincerely. Just get it straight in your head, and then let it flow. Impress with your willingness to repay, and your ability to do so. Let the loan officer know why you need the loan. If the reason convinces him that the loan will make your life better and more stable, that's in your favor.

Bring along backup documentation. Your WC-2 forms, or a Xerox of last year's income tax forms, will establish your earnings. But often it's your future earnings that are more important. If you can, get a recommendation from your boss that will indicate the stability of your job. If the boss says you're up for a raise, so much the better. If you have income from any other source than your job, bring along proof. For example, if you're renting out a room in your house, have Xeroxes of the rent checks made up. All this proves your *capacity* to pay.

Be prepared with character references. These should be people with whom you've had financial dealings: your family doctor, your dentist, your real estate broker, your lawyer, your accountant, your insurance broker, your securities broker, and so on. Have a list of names, addresses, and telephone numbers ready, and hand them over to the loan officer. Invite the loan officer to call these people while you're sitting there. Their testimony should help establish your *character*.

Be prepared with a list of your assets. Jewelry, paintings, books, workmen's tools, typewriters, autos, pickup trucks, securities, your home, land—anything. As you know, only a few kinds of assets are acceptable as collateral, but a list of what you own can be valuable in convincing the loan officer that you have the ability to acquire *capital*.

Ask for the maximum sum the bank will lend you. You know how to calculate that sum. You ask for maximum because the loan officer will probably agree to a lesser sum than what you ask for. Ask for less and you'll get even less. When you conclude your presentation, don't say, "Can I get a loan?" That requires a yes or no answer, and it could be no. Say instead, "What I would like is a loan for such-and-such an amount." The answer is likely to be, "I don't know if we can give you such-and-such, but we may be able to manage so-and-so." You're in!

But let's be realistic. If the computer says no, your chance of reversing the decision by a face-to-face meeting is small.

Meltzerism:
If your only chance of getting a loan is a personal interview with a loan officer, don't bank on it.

26. SUMMARY.

BERNARD MELTZER'S ADVICE ON GETTING YOUR LOAN APPROVED

Make the three C's—*character*, *capacity*, and *capital*—a way of life, and you'll not only get the loan or any other form of credit you need, but you'll also be a happier and more successful person.

PART II

Solving Your Buying Problems: How to Buy Your Home, Your Car, and Almost Anything on Credit

Chapter 6

The Best Way to Buy Is to Borrow

Do you realize how unusual the previous section is? I *really* talked about borrowing. You know everybody borrows, but nobody talks about it—*really* talks about it. It's like sex used to be. Everybody had sex, but nobody discussed it out in the open. Our attitude toward borrowing is still hush-hush. Recently a best-selling book was based on the idea that to beat inflation you had to borrow, but not one place in the book did it tell you *how* to borrow. Well, now you know *how* to borrow. And I think you have to know that before you can find the answers to your problems concerning buying. That's because all the major purchases you make in life will probably be made by borrowing. You'll borrow to buy a home and home repairs, to buy a car, to buy your kids' education or your own, to buy almost anything. Sometimes you'll borrow long-term—over as long as thirty-five years—and your interest charges will be enormous, as when you buy a house. Sometimes you'll borrow short-term—over as little as a few days—and you'll pay no interest charge at all, as when you use your credit card. But you will be buying through borrowing.

Borrowing is a natural outgrowth of the consumer society. We're all consumers, and borrowing makes it easier for us to consume. It also multiplies our consuming power. We buy three to four times as much as we would have bought had there been no credit system. In a sense, in a very real sense, our lives revolve around our purchases. Buying is at the very core of our feeling of accomplishment and well-being. So the problems of buying are among the key problems of life in America today. And those problems are related to borrowing. I want to talk to you about your buying problems in this connected sense.

Now, this is a lot different from the usual consumerism approach to buying which says, "Hey, watch out for all the ways you're being cheated, and let's bring in the government to control everything that's produced." There have been so many books, articles, and TV and radio broadcasts taking this approach that there is little or nothing new that can be added. My approach is different. It's based on true life experience—yours and mine. It says, "The American way has given us this remarkable credit system for getting us the highest standard of living in the history of the world. But each of us individually runs into problems on how to use this system to our best advantage." My approach says, "I don't want to solve your problems by changing the system. I want to work within the system to show you how to buy so you can be happiest with your purchases."

I'd like to expand on that just a bit. There's an old saying that tells you idealistic young men at twenty want to remake the world, and they continue trying at forty, only by then they know they can't do it. Many of our "young" idealists are now over forty, many much over forty, and they still keep trying even though they know they can't win. But what a lot of harm they cause! As for me, I know that the way to help people is not through mass projects—picketing, signing petitions, staging rallies. and so forth—but on a one-to-one basis. I don't want to change this country—it's a wonderful country. What I want to do is help you enjoy all its blessings. That's why I welcome writing this book, as I've welcomed my radio broadcasts for years, for the opportunity to talk to you on a one-to-one basis and pour out the knowledge and life experience which I've acquired not only from books but from the college of hard knocks from which I've earned many degrees.

Your problems exist in the world as it is, and my answers apply in that world. In this section are down-to-earth ways to get the things you want through borrowing. I will spend a great deal of space on buying a house, because it's not only the most important purchase of your life, it's also the most profitable investment you'll ever make. I spend a good deal of space, too, on buying your car, because it's an expensive piece of property that few people can get along without. And then I tell you about the man wonderful things you can do with your credit cards besides buying almost anything you want with them.

And, of course, I want you to remember all through Part II that when you borrow to buy, you'll be paying back with shrunken dollars—you're beating inflation. So, fellow consumers, let's go out and borrow to get all the good things of life we couldn't get otherwise—and pay back our debt with shrunken dollars. That amounts to saving money every time we buy—and that's a powerful way to make inflation work for you.

Chapter 7

Buying a House

IS THERE A DO-IT-YOURSELF WAY TO BUY A HOUSE?

There is not. To buy a house you need a group of experts to help you. You should pick them with care, because buying a house is the single most important purchase you will make in your life—far more important to most people than even buying a business. I know of one couple with a fixed amount of money who moved to Phoenix to start life anew. Their objects were to buy a house and to buy a business. But their first priority was buying a house. They had so little money left over that they had to settle for buying not quite the kind of big-volume business they had in mind. Not sound financially, experts would say. But from the emotional viewpoint, they had made the right decision. And in the long run it *was* smart financially, because a house is your best investment.

Now let's meet the experts who will help you buy a house. But before we do, a word of caution:

Meltzerism:
You can tell an expert not by the diplomas on the wall, but by the life experience on his face.

27. YOUR TEAM OF HOUSE-BUYING EXPERTS.

Let's take them one by one.

• *What you should know about your broker.* I've been using the pronoun "he" throughout this book because I don't believe in messing around with the English language, even though I have a deep respect for women's rights. But when I use a pronoun to substitute for "broker," it should be "she," because there are now many more women real estate brokers than there are men. This is one field where women have taken over. Some women have become outstanding successes earning in excess of $100,000 a year. Others work part-time, devoting the bulk of their time to their families, and these women average around $10,000 a year, which is a nice supplement to the family income. So when you meet a broker for the first time, the chances are you'll meet a woman.

What's her function? Well, if you're looking for a house, you could drive around trying to find For Sale signs, or you could search the town papers, or you could ask friends and neighbors, and it would take a lot of your time. Then you'd have to make appointments to see the house, and you'd have to give it a once-over yourself, and you'd have to negotiate price . . . and are you really equipped to do all that? Wouldn't it be easier to say to somebody, "Here's the kind of house I'm looking for and here's the kind of neighborhood I have in mind," then have that somebody come up with a list of houses that fit your specs, take you around in her car to see them, help you assess their suitability, and on and on? Well, that's roughly, very roughly, what a broker will do for you. And—this seems wonderful to a lot of people—she doesn't charge you a cent for her services.

It's not all that wonderful. The reason why is that she gets paid by the person who's trying to sell the house to you. That person has called up the broker and said, "I want to put my house on the market," and the broker has said, "Okay, I'll do my best to sell it for you *at the best possible price.*" And the broker certainly will, because she's going to get a percent of that price—very often it's 6 percent—as her fee. What the broker is is a saleswoman, and she's out to sell you a house. It would stand to reason that in the adversary relationship between buyer and seller, she's going to be in the seller's corner. So why do you go to a broker to buy a house? Because it's practically the only way it can be done.

Now once again, here's a situation that consumer advocates would scream about, and say, "Let's change the whole system. The consumer has a right to be represented by somebody who isn't acting for the seller," but the system works. It works in an American way—you won't buy anything unless it's right for you, and the broker knows that, so she only offers you a choice of houses which are right for you and are priced right. She also knows that selling houses is a word-of-mouth business; if she sells you an overpriced lemon, the word will get around, and she's going to get less and less business. I'm not going to pretend that there aren't unscrupulous brokers; there are. But in our free enterprise system, they tend to be driven out of the marketplace. Your big problem is to prevent yourself from being stung by one of them while they're still operating. The way to do that is to know enough about what you're buying so they can't pull the wool over your eyes. That's why I'm here—to give you that know-how.

All right, so you have to use a broker. What broker? You ask around and your friends say, "I used Doris Whitty and she was wonderful," so you call up Doris Whitty for an appointment, and you're on your way. But suppose some friends recommend Doris Whitty and others Joan Sprat, what do you do? You go around and visit both and you decide which one you like best, and that's how decisions are made in real life. That's fine, but I want to make one suggestion that will improve that decision. To understand my suggestion, you'll have to know a little bit about brokers.

All brokers have the same basic qualifications; they've passed an examination in order to get a license. But there are cram schools which prepare anybody for the state exam, so a license doesn't mean very much. Without life experience to back up paper knowledge, paper knowledge won't help you a bit anyway. Many brokers—some 250,000 of them—belong to a trade association called the National Association of Realtors (NAR) and are called Realtors, which is a trademark. Salespersons employed by a Realtor are called Realtor Associates. All Realtors and Associates are pledged to subscribe to the NAR's Code of Ethics, and most probably do. But a broker's being a Realtor rather than merely a real estate broker only means that she's paid dues to the association. A Realtor is not necessarily a more honest or efficient broker than a nonmember. Being a Realtor is not what counts; it's being *experienced* that does. If you were going about evaluating brokers in a Meltzer way, the first thing you would ask is, "How long have you been in business in this neck of the woods?" And if she says, "Six months," keep looking. Don't let your personal dislikes interfere with good common sense. If you like Doris Whitty better than Joan Sprat, but Doris has been around six months while Joan has been around sixteen years, go with Joan.

• *Services you can expect from an experienced broker*. Some women brokers will serve you coffee and cake. Great! Some of them will come over on the day you move in, and you're up to your neck in packing cases, and the kids are hungry, and your husband is due in from work in a few minutes, and bring you a home-cooked dinner for the entire family. Marvelous! But those are human services, expressions of friendship. You don't have to be a real estate professional to serve coffee and cake and cook a dinner. The kind of services I'm referring to are professional services—services which help you get the house that will make you the happiest. Here they are:

Your broker will tell you frankly if you can afford the kind of house you have in mind.   How can she know that? Simple—she draws a credit report on you. I emphasized before that the credit report is the keystone of happy living in the U.S.A. of the '80s, and here's a prime example. She draws the credit report for two reasons. The first is that she wants to know if you can pay for the kind of house you specify (why should she be running around and knocking herself out only to find you haven't got the dough to close the deal?); and the second is she genuinely wants to find the best house you can get for the money you can realistically spend. What she'll do is point out to you what's available in your price range. That will save you a lot of time, and a lot of disappointments. No sense in seeing a house, getting your heart set on it, then finding it's way out of reach.

Your broker will help you find out what kind of a house you really want.   "What do you mean by that?" I'm often asked. "If my husband and I don't know what kind of a house we want, who does?" Granted. But sometimes people have trouble making what they want quite clear to the broker. So the broker will go through a checklist, asking you questions like: "What are you looking for in a house? Space? A good neighborhood? Peace and quiet? Closeness to the city? Nearness to schools, shopping centers, the water, churches?" She'll ask, "What style of house do you have in mind? What kind of construction? How many bedrooms do you need? Do you need a big kitchen? How much ground would you like? Do you want rooms with a separate entrance for your aging parents?" And on and on. It's a very reasonable approach. You're going to live in that house for an awfully long time. You should know clearly what you want even before you go shopping for it.

Your broker will search not only her own listings but also other brokers' listings to find the house that's right for you.   That means she has to share her commission, but she gets it back in the long run because other brokers make use of her listings. The more listings a broker has available to her, the better chance you have of getting the house you want.

Your broker will keep you up-to-date on her progress.   One of the worst things that can happen to you when you're house hunting through a broker is being left in the dark. The phone should be ringing constantly and you should be going out time after time with the broker to see houses.

Your broker will help you make up your mind about a house, but she won't try to sell you on something you don't want. Sometimes the broker searches and searches and just can't get a house with all of your specifications. So it comes down to a decision on whether you want house A with the extra bedroom or house B with the patio. It's a kind of thing you can settle sometimes by finding a sympathetic listener, and pouring out your pros and cons until *you* come to a decision. The broker could be that listener. Or the broker could be helpful in a technical way, drawing on her store of experience.

Take the case of Billy and Esther Powell. Esther told me that they found this lovely house with "just a darling divider wall between the living room and the dining room. But it wasn't just a wall, it was a lovely, lovely bookcase." The couple had seen another house which they also liked. "But," Esther said, "I just fell in love with the bookcase. I said to the owner, 'I want this house because I don't know how I'm going to live without that bookcase divider.' But the owner said to me, 'I can understand just how you feel, because I wouldn't part with that bookcase for all the oil in Saudi Arabia. It doesn't go with the house. I'm taking it with me.'" Esther called her broker, told her the whole story, and told her how bitterly disappointed she was. "I guess," she said to the broker, "We'll have to take the other house." "Not if you have your heart set on the house with the bookcase," the broker said to her; and then explained that because the bookcase was really part of the wall, not a separate fixture, it was considered by law to be part of the house, and it could not be taken out. "Why," the broker said, "if they took out the bookcase, you would be moving in with a big hole where the wall should have been." The broker brought the facts to the attention of the owner, who didn't know the law either, and finally everything was straightened out. The bookcase-divider remained, and Billy and Esther Powell got the house they wanted.

Your broker will give you a reasonable projection of the neighborhood's future. To my mind the most important single factor in choosing a house is neighborhood. Obviously, you're not going to move into a bad neighborhood. But neighborhoods, as we all know, often from our own bitter experience, sometimes decline. You can drive through a neighborhood and get the impression that this is just the place you want to live in for the rest of your life. But how do you know it's going to stay that way? How do you know that at the very moment you decide to buy a house, the property right on the other side of the road hasn't been sold to a promoter who's going to build a discotheque, or an electronic games arcade, or an X-rated-movie house? How do you know that the county supervisor isn't planning right now to rip up that pleasant country lane that abuts the property you have in mind and turn it into a highway? How do you know that undesirable tenants haven't been moving into the neighborhood in growing numbers? How do you know that the school which looks so modern and spic-and-span on the outside isn't going downhill with no money for maintenance and teachers? And how do you know that real estate taxes, which seem in line now, aren't going to skyrocket next year, and the year after, and so on? You can't know these things. But a broker who knows the neighborhood intimately does know these things, and she should tell you.

Your broker should arrange for all the experts you need, and for your financing if you request it.   Consumer advocates advise shopping around for your own experts and your own mortgage, and while that's mathematically good advice, let's temper it with life experience. Most of us don't even know where to go to find experts, let alone how to evaluate them when we find them. You *could* learn how to do it. But why bother when an experienced broker has the names of experts at her fingertips? What you can do, though, is take a hard look at her recommendations before you go along with them. I'll tell you how to do that:

• *What you should know about your appraiser. Caveat emptor* is an old Latin phrase, and it was probably invented by an ancient Roman businessman, because it means "Let the buyer beware." And that phrase applies more to buying a house than it does to any other kind of consumer purchase. That's because on most other consumer purchases you have a "warranty of fitness," implied or explicit—which in plain English means if it's a lemon you can exchange it, get your money back, or have it fixed. But not when you buy a used house. Once you've bought it as is and you find defects in it, you're stuck with it.

So it's a good idea to have the house given a good once-over by somebody who knows about houses. Such a person is called an appraiser, and he'll tell you two things: What's wrong with the house, and what the house is worth. Let's take what's wrong with the house first. There's no way in the world that you could look at a house and be certain the roof doesn't leak, the basement doesn't flood, the heating and cooling units aren't efficient, the water pressure isn't too low, the sewer system isn't a disgrace, the electric circuitry isn't dangerous, and so on. Would you be able to pass judgment on the basic structure—the foundation, the walls, the girders, the columns, the sills, the joists, the floors, and so on? I don't think so. And if you're worried about termites, would you be able to tell whether they were hiding in the woodwork? No way. But the appraiser can. What he finds out will come in handy when you get around to the contract, which I'll discuss in a little while. On the basis of what he finds, and a lot of other factors, he'll come up with a market price for the house. If it's in line with the asking price, you know you may have a good buy. But if it's out of line—if the asking price is much higher or much lower—you're in trouble. Get your broker to do some explaining before you go ahead with the deal.

How do you know you've got an appraiser you can trust? Sometimes your real estate broker can double as an appraiser. I was both. If you trust your real estate broker as a broker, and he tells you he's a qualified appraiser, and has been appraising property to everybody's satisfaction for years, I think you can trust him or her as an appraiser, too. If your broker suggests an appraiser, ask, "What are his qualifications?" It's good news if she says the appraiser she has in mind is a member of the American Institute of Real Estate Appraisers. That means he meets the standards of the institute and has passed an examination, and has the right to put M.A.I. (Member of the Appraisal Institute), R.M. (Residential Member), or S.R.A. (Senior Residential Appraiser) after his name. But nothing takes the place of life experience, and if your broker tells you the appraiser she's recommending has only been at his job for a short while, ask for somebody experienced instead. The kind of appraiser I like to see is a retired construction expert. *He* knows what it's all about. I know that for a fact because I'm a construction expert myself.

• *What you should know about your lawyer.* Before the house is yours, you're going to be dealing with such things as—now I'm going to reel off a number of legal terms, and you see whether you know the ins and outs of all of them—*binders . . . real estate contracts . . . deposits . . . escrows . . . mortgages . . . titles . . . deeds . . .* had enough? Of course you're no expert in the meaning of these words unless you're a real estate lawyer or unless you made it your business to learn all about them. Most of us don't qualify on either count. So it looks like you're going to need a lawyer.

That's not always true. In California there are companies—escrow and title companies—that handle all the details of house buying *for* you, and there's not a lawyer in sight. Some housing development builders have in the past provided the same kind of service. There are even some people with strong do-it-yourself feelings who go through all the steps of house buying without *any* experts. How does all this work out? When experienced companies or builders take over for you, it usually works out well. When you do it yourself, you could live happily ever after, or you could be moving into a disaster.

It's customary almost everywhere (except in California) to have a lawyer in when buying a house. He knows how to handle all the documents so you're not trapped into buying anything you don't want to buy, or committing yourself to anything you don't want to be committed to, or paying for anything you don't want to pay for, or being stuck with faulty construction. But—and here's a big but—the lawyer can't tell you about the pitfalls in buying a house; he can only write ways of avoiding them into the documents after *you tell him* what pitfalls *you* discovered and what *you* want to do about them. He can also negotiate with the seller's lawyer, or the seller, about what you want concerning these pitfalls and what the seller is willing to give. All this will become much clearer as we get into the actual steps for buying a house later on.

The point is, a lawyer is not a real estate expert. He doesn't take the place of your broker or your appraiser; *they* are the people who point out the pitfalls to you and tell you what to do about them. The lawyer makes what you want to do legal and binding. Don't rely on a lawyer if he's a corporation lawyer, or a criminal lawyer, or any other kind of a lawyer except a real estate lawyer. Real estate law is so complex, and there's so much detail involved, that I could write a dozen books on it and still not even begin to cover it all. If you don't know a reliable and experienced real estate lawyer—and once again, *experience* is the key word—then ask your broker. She'll be able to recommend one to you.

• *What you should know about your "mortgage counselor."* There's no such animal as a "mortgage counselor." But there are people who can give you advice on the best kind of mortgage. One of those people is the mortgage officer at your bank. Another is your broker. And there are mortgage brokers who shop for the best mortgage for you, and charge you a fee for the service. Sometimes, but not always, your lawyer can be of help.

Getting the right mortgage is a pretty complex and detailed subject, and you and I will get into it in a separate section. Once you've read that section, I think the only need you'll have of a mortgage counselor is to dot the i's and cross the t's.

So that's your team of experts: a broker, an appraiser, a lawyer, and a mortgage counselor. Now let's see how they are useful to you as you take—

28. SIX STEPS TO OWNING YOUR OWN HOME.

• *Step 1: The binder.* Here's the situation: Your broker has found the house that's right for you. You're happy with it. You like the price. You've made up your mind. You say to the seller, "Okay, I want it." The seller says, "You've got it. Now let's get a contract drawn up." You shake hands, and you've got yourself a deal. Are you really committed to buy the house, and is the seller really committed to sell it, on the basis of a handclasp agreement? The answer is, "Legally, yes—*in most states.*"

I emphasize *in most states* because I want to digress for a moment and talk about real estate law, or as it's more properly called, "real property law," as it applies across the nation. There is no national real estate code. Each state makes up its own laws. The real estate laws in most states are very complicated, and you can get to know them in only two ways. If you're a lawyer you have to specialize in this field—and I mean *really* specialize. You'll have to spend years in law libraries digging out all the loopholes and escape clauses and booby traps. If you're a broker you have to gain years and years of experience on the firing line. Now remember, lawyers don't make real estate deals; they just make the deals legal. Brokers make the deals, and they have to apply the law every day, day in and day out, for the benefit of their clients. "Ninety-nine percent of all real estate deals . . . require expertise from the broker who had to work his way through the financial jungle where the real issues are," says Howard Goldson; and he should know, because he's the counsel to the Long Island Board of Realtors. So for *detailed* guidance on buying or selling a house, go to brokers and/or lawyers in the state where the transaction is taking place.

"Now, wait a minute, Dr. Meltzer," I can hear you saying. "If real estate laws are so tricky and they differ from state to state, how can you tell me anything about my real estate problems? Why don't I just go to my broker or my lawyer for advice and say, 'Goodbye, Dr. Meltzer'?" You know, I had a real-life experience revolving around a question just like yours. I'll tell it to you, and in that way you'll get a good grasp of the answer.

I was running a column on real estate in a Philadelphia paper, much like the column I'm now running in the *Daily News* in New York, and I get it into my head that this kind of information I'm writing about is so useful that people should be interested in it all over the nation, not just in Philadelphia. So I go to the office of a national newspaper syndicate, a real giant that services thousands of newspapers from the Canadian border to the Mexican border and from the Atlantic Coast to the shores of the Pacific, and I sit down with the editor, and I tell him what's on my mind. Do you know what he says to me? He says, "Meltzer, you should have your head examined. How can you do a national column on real estate when the laws are different in every state? You'll have to sit down and research and write fifty different columns each week, one for each state. It's ridiculous!" No sale. So what I do is as follows:

I take the same column I'm doing in Philadelphia, and I go to newspapers in New Jersey, and one by one I sell them on using the column. Two different states but the same column. The columns are so popular that soon I get a call from the editor of the syndicate, and he says to me, "Bernie"—it's "Bernie" now, not "Meltzer"—"Bernie, you know who should have his head examined? Me." And I say, "Why?" And he says, "Because I didn't realize what you were going to do. Your columns are great. And they can be used in any state."

What I had done was this: I talked about basic rules and procedures that are *alike* in every state. They're so fundamental that they can serve as sound and secure guidelines when you buy a house in any state. So before you say, "Goodbye, Dr. Meltzer," and rush off to your broker and lawyer, read on. When you get to using those experts, you'll know how to get the best out of them.

And while I'm still digressing, I want to add one thing. It's about lawyers. I'm sometimes accused of talking lawyers down, but that's not true. All I say is, a lawyer is trained to be an expert in the law; he's not trained to be an expert in everything, and certainly he's not trained to be an expert in real estate—in real estate *law,* maybe, but in the everyday practice of real estate, the ins and outs of buying and selling, the financial arrangements, and so on, he's no expert. The trouble with a lot of people is, they regard lawyers as knowing everything. Got a problem, go see a lawyer. And that brings me to another—

Meltzerism:
If you have a legal *problem, see a lawyer. If you have any other kind of problem, don't.*

Now to get back to the handclasp agreement to buy a house. Yes, it can be binding on both parties. But how can you prove a verbal agreement in the event the seller changes his mind; or how can he prove it, for that matter, if you change your mind? It's a virtual impossibility. So what happens is, you're asked to sign a paper that *is* more binding—and, naturally, that paper is called a binder.

The funny thing about a binder is that it doesn't really bind. It's an agreement to agree. It's supposed to state that you and the seller have agreed on the sale of his house at such-and-such a price, and you've also agreed to sign a contract to that effect in so-and-so many days. To show good faith, you put up a small sum of money. That money is sometimes called "earnest money," because "earnest" means showing good faith. It's understood that if you don't sign the contract in so-and-so many days, the deal is off, and the money you put up is returned to you.

"If either party can call the deal off," I'm asked now and then, "what good's the binder?" Look at it this way: A binder is like a deposit on some item you want a storekeeper to put aside for you. The deposit shows your intent to buy; and when the storekeeper takes it, that shows his intent to sell the item to you and to nobody else. But how many times do you go into the store and say, "I'm so sorry, but I just can't buy the item at this time, and I'd like to have my deposit back"—and get it? And how many times does the storekeeper say, "Oh, I'm sorry, my clerk sold it by mistake, so here's your deposit back"? A binder is a loose arrangement to help keep the deal from falling through while the contract is being drawn up.

Another question that arises is: "What if the seller spends my earnest money, and doesn't have it when I want it back?" Your broker knows that's always a possibility, so he arranges that the money be placed in escrow. "Escrow" means held by a third party. Your broker is a third party, and he usually has an escrow fund account at his bank for just such transactions. Ninety-nine point nine percent of brokers in this country are honest, so you'll have no trouble getting your money back.

The binder leaves you a certain number of days to think the deal over; and should you decide you don't want the house after all, you get your money back and no harm done. You have not signed a contract, and you're off the hook. But be careful—some so-called binders *are* contracts. They contain items which should not appear in a binder, but always appear in a contract, such as:

1. How much you're going to pay.
2. When you're going to pay it.
3. A detailed description of the property.
4. All items that are not real property—that is to say, all items which are not considered part of the building and grounds (remember the

bookcase-divider?)—which are included in the sale (garden statuary, drapes, that kind of thing).

5. Who pays certain costs, like taxes and insurance.

6. When you can take possession.

7. Assurance that you'll be supplied with a title warranty. (We'll get into that when we discuss the contract.)

8. What kind of deed you're going to get. (Some kinds of deeds are worthless, and I'll tell you why when we get into the contract.)

9. What happens if for any reason you can't get financing.

10. What happens to the escrow money in case you can't get financing.

When you sign a so-called binder containing these items, what you're signing is really a contract. And a contract *is* binding. Should you try to get out of it, you could be heading for trouble. Take the case of the Siegels—

They lived in a pleasant suburb of Cleveland. But, as has been happening all over the nation, the kind of crime that once was restricted to the big cities spread to the Siegels' neighborhood. And when it came, it came with a vengeance. In less than a month, there were three muggings, four burglaries (in one of them a seventy-two-year-old woman was stabbed and beaten), and two rapes. The Siegels had two teenage daughters, so they panicked, and decided to get out of there, and get out of there fast. They were in such a hurry that they didn't bother to shop around for a broker to get them a house farther away from the city; they let their fingers do the walking and picked a broker at random from the Yellow Pages. She happened to have a lot of push, and access to good listings; and inside of two weeks, she had the Siegels a house in a neighborhood relatively free of crime. She called the Siegels and said, "I've even got the binder signed by Mr. DeAngelo"—he was the seller—"and I'll come right over for your signature and a check." After the Siegels signed the binder and handed over the check, Ed Siegel said to the broker, "What happens if we change our mind?" By this time the panic was subsiding, the police had caught most of the hoodlums, things had quieted down; and, after all, the Siegels had lived in this house for nearly sixteen years, it was their home. "If you change your mind, this is just a binder," the broker said. "You'll get your money back, and the deal's off. No problem."

But it was a problem. That was because the broker, who was inexperienced, used a binder form which she had bought in a stationery store. It was a form that contained blanks for all the items I just listed. It wasn't a binder at all; it was a contract. When the Siegels changed their minds and told the broker, she came back with the bad news: "Mr. DeAngelo says he's not going to let you out of it. He says you're committed and you have to buy the house." "No way we'll do it," the Siegels told her. "No way at all." So DeAngelo took it to court, and the litigation went on for about a year, and in the end the judge held the Siegels had signed not a binder but a contract, and the Siegels were obliged to buy the house. The Siegels then made a settlement with DeAngelo—they didn't actually buy the house, but it did cost them a wad of dough—and the matter was closed.

What's the moral of this story? Just follow—

BERNARD MELTZER'S ADVICE ON WHEN TO BRING IN A LAWYER WHEN YOU'RE BUYING A HOUSE

Bring him in just as soon as the binder is ready. He'll know whether it's a true binder or a contract.

• *Step 2: The inspection.* You want to be sure you're moving into a house you can live in without going into hock for repairs. This is when you call in the appraiser (who may be assisted by other inspection specialists). If things have to be done by the seller to be sure the house is livable, he'll tell you. You can check on the appraiser's competence by getting a copy of the free booklet *Basic Housing Inspection* (write HEW, Room 1587, Parklawn Building, 5600 Fisher's Lane, Rockville, MD 20852) and seeing if the appraiser inspected everything the government experts who wrote the booklet think ought to be inspected.

You have to get the inspection done fast, because you usually have only ten days between the time you sign the binder and the time you're required to sign the contract. To expedite things, tell the appraiser, "Don't worry about a written report if that means a delay. Give me the information on the phone, and then follow it up with a written report." Also, remember he will tell you what he thinks the property is worth. If it's in line with the price you agreed on, fine. But if that price is much higher than the appraised price, have a talk with your broker. You may be able to knock the price down appreciably.

After the inspection, you can tell the lawyer what you want done before you move in—repairs to the heating system or termite inspection, for example—and after negotiation with the seller, he'll see that all or most of what you want is properly incorporated in the contract. Some lawyers will tell you that you can have the inspection done after the contract. They argue that you have nothing to worry about because they'll include a clause in the contract which says the deal is off if there's an unsatisfactory inspection report. But to my mind it makes no sense to make a deal, then break it and start negotiations all over again, when it's so much easier to get the inspection and the negotiations done *before* the contract is signed.

• *Step 3: The contract.*   This is probably the most important document you'll sign in your life. Usually the contract will come to you as a printed form with blanks filled in, and will be presented to you by the realtor. State realtor associations through long experience have worked out forms which fit most any house-purchasing transaction. Some state bar associations also offer prepared stock contracts which have proved serviceable. But don't think that because a contract comes to you printed it's a "standard" contract. There's no such thing. Every agreement to buy a house is a very special one, and must be tailored to your needs, with the consent of the seller. Let's go over the clauses of a typical contract.

1. The date, the name of the seller, and your name.

2. The legal description of the property.   The street address is not enough. What is required here is a survey of the property made by a surveyor. The seller usually has such a survey available.

3. Personal property included in the sale.   Built-in fixtures, such as commodes, light fixtures, and sinks, are considered part of the house, and need not be listed. But what about carpets? The basketball hoop in the yard? Air conditioners? The vegetable garden? When there's some doubt about what's a fixture, the best thing to do is to decide with the seller what personal property is included in the sale, then have your lawyer write the agreement into the contract.

4. Purchase price and how it is payable.   This brings up the whole subject of mortgages, which is so involved that I'm going to talk about it in a special section. But one thing must be made clear here, and that is: If you can't get a satisfactory mortgage within a specified time, the deal is off. While you're searching for a mortgage, the seller would like you to put up a deposit, which he'd like to keep if you can't find a mortgage. The deposit is not to be confused with earnest money, and it can be a considerable sum. So work out with the seller whether it's returnable or not, and if you come to a satisfactory agreement, have your lawyer include it in the contract. Beginning to get the idea of how complicated a contract for the sale of a house can be? It's going to get even more complicated. But hang on, my explanation will stay simple—and this is the stuff you just *have* to know to get the best deal.

5. *Abstract of title.*   You've heard the phrase "You now have title to the property." That means the property is yours to use as you please within certain limitations. Those limitations may be provided by zoning laws, and by the deed itself. (More about the deed in a little while.) When you have title to a property, you can sell it or mortgage it. So you want to be sure the seller *does* have title to the property before *you* buy it, so you can mortgage it now, and sell it later if you wish.

Now, it's not likely that the seller is trying to palm off a piece of property to which he doesn't have title. But—and this happens frequently—the title may be "clouded." That means there may be claims on the title. What kinds of claims? How about a missing heir who suddenly pops up? How about liens (rights to the property in lieu of payments of debts)? How about typographical errors in former descriptions of the property, so that the title the seller has is for a piece of property that doesn't really exist? How about a former owner's not signing a deed (a deed is the document which actually transfers title from one person to another), so the present owner's claims to the title can be disputed on a technicality? And how about a forged deed? Do you know how many different kinds of claims can be made against a title? According to the Federal Housing Administration, about a thousand!

That's why the contract calls for the seller to supply you with an "abstract of title." That means that somebody—in practice, a title company—searches the public records and comes up with a history of the title. That's called a title search. Then the result of the title search is set down in a report which is called an abstract of title. The title search may uncover some of the thousand or so claims that can cloud the title. If it does, then the seller must clear the title before the contract can take effect.

But that's not good enough for mortgage officers at banks, and it's not good enough for the FHA (Federal Housing Administration), which guarantees mortgages. How can they know that the title search was complete? Isn't it possible that some hidden claims can surface after the mortgage has been granted? They can't know that the search was complete; and, yes, hidden claims can surface. So what banks and the FHA require before they can respectively grant or guarantee a mortgage is title insurance. What this kind of insurance does is guarantee that once the title passes to you, if there are claims against it you will not be held accountable. If the matter goes to court, the insurance company will defend and pay all legal expenses. If the insurance company loses, it will pay all claims. You can't lose, and neither can the mortgage holders.

Who pays for title insurance, you or the seller? That's a matter for horse trading. If you can get the seller to agree to pay, get your lawyer to put it in the contract.

6. *Up-to-the-minute survey.* The property has already been legally described, but how do you know that the description matches the actual property? You don't. The only way to know is to get an up-to-the-minute survey. It may show what realtors call "encroachments"—really a theft of property by a neighbor. For example, the surveyor may find that a neighbor's fence is two feet inside the property you're about to buy. Who pays for the survey? Try to get the seller to do it, and have your lawyer specify it in the contract. And what if there are encroachments? Have your lawyer also specify that they must be removed in such-and-such a time (usually thirty days).

7. *Termite inspection and other types of special inspection.* Your appraiser has made a general inspection of the house and indicated areas where defects must be corrected. Have your lawyer indicate that these defects must be corrected by the seller in a certain time (usually thirty days). Your appraiser may have indicated that specialists be brought in to examine roofing, plumbing, wiring, appliances, and other parts of the property. He may also have recommended that a termite inspector be brought in. Once again, try to have the seller assume the charges for these special inspections; and make that a part of the contract. Should defects turn up as a result of the inspections, have the contract state that they must be set right within the time you specify (usually thirty days).

8. *Deed.* The contract states that at the closing (and we'll discuss the closing in some detail) you will receive the deed to the property. As you know, that means the property is really yours. But you must be careful about the deed, because there are three kinds of deeds, and only one provides complete protection. Let's first look at the two kinds of deeds that are tricky.

The quit-claim deed, when you translate all the legal gobbledegook, is a statement by the seller which says, "I don't know if I own this property, and I don't know if I have any rights to it at all, but whatever ownership I have in it, whatever rights I have to it, are yours." When you get that kind of deed you know the owner believes the title is clouded and he wants to protect himself from lawsuits. But you don't want to have anything to do with a clouded title. Stay away from a quit-claim deed.

The bargain and sale deed says in essence that the seller has a marketable title and he's transferring it to you. What if it isn't a marketable title? Your hard luck. Stay away from this kind of deed.

A full covenant and warranty deed is what you want. In this deed the seller says, "I promise and guarantee that you will enjoy the ownership of this property, and you can use it as you see fit within the limitations of the deed, and no one will dispute your rights, and no one will interfere with them. If anybody makes a claim on the title, I'll be financially responsible for any loss or damage to you." Now you can understand why this document is called the deed of "quiet enjoyment."

A deed describes the property with precision. The up-to-the-minute survey is incorporated into the description.

9. Expenses. Here's where your lawyer specifies all the items the seller has to pay for. In addition to those we've already talked about, there are costs of the preparation of the deed, revenue stamps on the deed, real estate commission, stamps and expenses for the mortgage and note, and expenses for recording the mortgage. You'll try to get away with as few expenses as possible, but whatever they are, they have to be listed as well.

10. Taxes and insurance. An arrangement is made to prorate taxes and insurance for the current year. Obviously you don't want to be stuck with a full year's burden of these expenses if you'll have occupancy for only a few months of the year.

11. Dates of closing and occupancy. You'll want to know exactly when the house becomes yours (closing date), and when you can move in, which may not be the same date. Not infrequently, the closing will occur before you move in. That's a courtesy gesture on your part to give the seller a chance to move out at an appropriate time.

12. Damage to the property. What happens if after you've signed the contract and before you receive the deed, the house is damaged, say by fire or flood or vandalism? The contract has to state that that's the seller's hard luck, not yours. The seller is given a certain time to restore the house to your satisfaction (usually sixty days) or the deal is off.

13. Deposit. The seller acknowledges receipt of the deposit. The deposit is placed in escrow.

14. Signatures. The seller affixes his signature, and you do likewise. If the seller is really more than one person—say a man and wife—both signatures are required; and if you and your wife are buying, both your signatures are needed as well.

So that's a bird's-eye view of the contract. It will help you in two ways. The first is, now you know what you can ask for and what you should get in a contract that's right for you. The second is, you can talk intelligently with your lawyer.

• *Step 4: The mortgage.*   Before I go into the specifics about mortgages and what they cost and so on, I want to talk a little bit about what a mortgage means, and what it has meant, to the American way of life. One of the wonderful parts of the American dream is the belief that you, I, everybody can own a home. Until the surge of high mortgage rates, this was a part of the dream that came true for millions of Americans. Statistics vary depending on the source, but some figures show that 80 percent of American families own their own homes. And even now with 18 percent mortgages *plus* costs, the dream persists; and all sorts of ways are being figured out to put mortgages in the hands of people—especially couples starting out in life—who need them. (I'll talk about some of those ways in this Step.)

But buying a home with a mortgage wasn't always part of the dream, nor was it part of the American way of life. Abe Lincoln's father, for example, didn't buy a house; he didn't even buy a piece of land. What he did was roam around the wilderness of Kentucky and Illinois until he found a suitable place near a clear stream. He took out his ax, cleared the ground, and used the trees to build a log cabin. At the same time, along the built-up East Coast of the nation—in New York, Virginia, New England, Maryland, the Carolinas, and New Jersey—a lot of people rented homes, and some bought them. I say, *some*—because most people simply couldn't afford to buy. Let me explain: The cost of a house in those days was five to ten times an average person's annual income. (Up until very recently it was only two and a half to three times.) There was no financing in those days, and you had to pay cash. You saved and saved and saved until you were able to buy a house; and some families never could save up enough.

Then, as you know, savings banks and savings and loan associations came into the picture, and made mortgages available. But still you had to be fairly well off to afford a house. The length of most mortgages was four to five years, which meant big monthly payments, and the interest was 6 percent, laughably low today, but in those days a strain on all budgets except those of the rich and the upper middle class. It wasn't until 1934, when FDR founded the Federal Housing Administration (FHA), that the dream of a house for every American family became a reality. Under the FHA, mortgages were extended to thirty and thirty-five years, monthly payments dipped to wonderfully easy-to-pay amounts, and interest rates were much lower than those at conventional mortgage sources. Today, an FHA-guaranteed mortgage is still a bargain.

So you can see what a mortgage means, and has meant, to the American way of life. It's a document that has made America a land of homeowners, and will continue to make America a land of homeowners forever. Look at a mortgage that way, and you'll agree with me that it's one of the great inventions of the human mind. And remember, it's a form of borrowing. Borrowing, as I've said before, is the keystone of consumer happiness in our times; and the mortgage is the most important form of borrowing.

Now, let's go into specifics—the types of mortgages.

The FHA mortgage. Strictly speaking, this should be called an FHA-*insured* mortgage, because the FHA doesn't make a mortgage to you; it insures the mortgage you get from a conventional mortgage source, like a bank. To get an FHA mortgage, you go to your bank and tell the mortgage officer that you want such a mortgage. You never go to the FHA directly. If you've already signed the contract, show it to the mortgage officer. If you haven't signed the contract yet, tell him how much you're paying for the house. He'll get a detailed statement from you, and he'll pass it through for credit check. Even though the bank can't lose because the loan is insured by the FHA, nevertheless they won't accept your request if you're a bad credit risk. If a bank ran up a record of accepting bad credit risks, the FHA would have a serious talk with the bank president; but this has never happened. So don't think that just because these mortgages are backed up by the U.S. government you can get one if your credit rating is a 9.

Once you get by the credit check, the FHA arranges for an appraisal of the house; they're not going to give you a mortgage on a house you're about to pay $100,000 for when their appraisal shows it's only worth $60,000. Better be sure of the appraisal value before you apply for an FHA mortgage. The FHA also arranges for an inspection of the house—and that's a tough inspection, because FHA standards are very, very high. If the house doesn't pass the inspection, no deal. The FHA is also very particular about where the house is located. If it's in the wrong neighborhood, no deal. And unless title is unquestionably clear, and you have no liability for claims that could be made against you, no deal. What's more, there's a lot of red tape associated with FHA mortgages, and you have to wait and wait until you get one.

There are more disadvantages. The FHA has its own mortgage form, and no way—*no way*—are you permitted to change even a single "whereas" or "wherefore." The forms of conventional mortgage sources are flexible to some degree, and can be altered to meet your specific needs. On FHA mortgages you're required to pay one-twelfth of the estimated yearly taxes and insurance with each monthly mortgage payment. The money is then placed in escrow, and then at the end of the year, or whenever tax and insurance payments are due, the mortgage holder pays your taxes and insurance for you. The FHA simply doesn't trust you to make these two vital payments. This is somewhat unfair to you, because you could have had the use of that money to invest in any way you pleased for the course of a year.

What *is* attractive about an FHA mortgage is: First, you can stretch out payments for thirty to thirty-five years. Second, your down payment is extremely low—3 percent of the first $25,000 of appraised value plus 5 percent of the appraised value over $25,000. So on an $80,000 home, down payment would amount to only $3,500. On a conventional mortgage the down payment is usually 20 percent, and would amount to $16,000. That's quite a difference! But there's a fly in the ointment. The FHA will not permit you to borrow that $3,500 or any part of it. Unless you have the money for the down payment, they won't grant you the mortgage. The interest rate on an FHA mortgage is usually lower than you can get anywhere else, but in practice, it may not be. To make up the difference between the low interest rate and the going interest rate, bankers add "points." I'd like to explain this "point" system in some detail, because it's a way bankers and other mortgage sources get around all government-imposed ceilings on mortgage interest.

A point is equal to 1 percent of the face value of the mortgage. On a $60,000 mortgage, 1 point would equal $600, 5 points would equal $3,000, 10 points would equal $6,000, and so on. The total value of the points is deducted from your mortgage at the beginning. So if the banker charges 10 points on a mortgage of $60,000, you get only $54,000. But you pay back $60,000 *and* interest on the $60,000. This raises your real interest rate, so on an FHA mortgage you could end up paying an interest rate as high as or higher than you would if you had taken out a conventional mortgage.

What interest rates prevail at the FHA changes rapidly these days. To stay abreast of them, ask your mortgage officer, or write FHA, Department of Housing and Urban Development, 451 7th Street, S.W., Washington, DC 20410. So far as what points your bank will add, see your mortgage officer.

The VA mortgage is guaranteed by the Veterans Administration and is available to certain eligible veterans. This kind of mortgage was established through the Serviceman's Readjustment Act of 1944, and if you can get one (they're not too easy to get), you're in luck. Here's how to count your blessings. *One:* You don't have to make any down payment at all. The mortgage covers the full payment of the appraised value of the house. *Two:* You can pay off all or part of the loan faster than required without paying a penalty. Bankers don't like you to pay off fast because they lose interest, so most mortgages contain a provision which says you have to pay a penalty—a certain percentage of the mortgage—in the event you prepay. Even FHA mortgages contain that provision. *Three:* You have thirty to thirty-five years to pay off, so your monthly payments are low. *Four:* Interest rates are lower. You can find out what they are currently by dropping a card to the Veterans Administration, Washington, DC 20420. But watch out for points. *Five:* If you run into difficulty making payments, the VA will come to your rescue to the extent that it will help you work out some way of making lesser payments to the bank until you can get on your feet.

As when getting an FHA mortgage, you start by talking with the mortgage officer at your bank, or you can write to the Veterans Administration for details.

FmHA mortgage. If you're in your sixties, and if your income is lower than the national average, there's a chance you can qualify for these low-cost mortgages, provided you live in a rural area or a small town. FmHA stands for the Farmers Home Administration, and what it does is guarantee your mortgage. You go about getting this kind of mortgage much as you would go about getting a VA or FHA mortgage —by going in and talking to the mortgage officer of your bank. Mortgages run up to thirty-three years, and the interest rates are determined by what your income is and how many dependents you have. You can get the actual figures, which like all other rates these days fluctuate too rapidly to set down in permanent print, by writing Farmers Home Administration, Department of Agriculture, Washington, DC 20250.

The conventional mortgage. Now, all three types of mortgages which I've discussed so far—FHA, VA, and FmHA—are government-controlled, even though the mortgages are actually granted by private enterprise. They serve a purpose—they make mortgages available to the aging, the low-income groups, and to the men and women who have contributed parts of their lives to the defense of our country and the free world. For the rest of us, conventional mortgages are available from a number of sources, as you already know. The great majority of American mortgages come from these sources, so let's take a look at them—and let's look at how conventional mortgages are changing to meet the challenge of interest rates that are going through the ceiling.

I've already told you where you can get conventional mortgages and the advantages of one kind of mortgage source over another. Now I'd like to talk to you about the extremely high interest rates and what happens when they're applied to the high costs of today's house.

The house that an average family of four would be happy in costs in today's market about $69,000—and it may have gone higher since this book went to press. That's a lot of money, especially if the family is young. A standard 20 percent down payment comes to $13,800—enough to wipe out a young family's savings. Many young people come to me and tell me they just can't afford it. Others say they have to borrow from their relatives and they hate to do it. Still others, who say to me that "they're one big down payment away" from owning a home, "and that's far, far away," feel they're not going to live as well as their parents—a frightening prospect, and so un-American in attitude. Part of the American Dream is that every generation should—and will—live better than the one before. For generation after generation, that part of the dream has come true. We must not let it die.

That's why all over the country mortgage experts are racking their brains to find new ways to help people buy their own homes. The sum of their efforts is called "creative selling." I don't like the name, and I'll tell you why: It implies that the mortgage people are selling you something they couldn't sell otherwise, just to put profits in their pockets. There's nothing wrong with profits, but the human aspect must be considered, too. I'd like to think these experts are trying to find new ways to help people buy what they want so that more and more people can be happier. In that way everybody profits. So what *I'd* like to call the new ideas in mortgaging is "creative buying."

But before we go into creative buying, let's see how bad the situation really is. Some statistics: A decade ago, one out of every three mortgages went to a first-time buyer. Today, the figure is one out of five. From 1977 to 1979, the overall consumer price index, a sound measure of inflation, rose by about 32 percent. During that same time, the cost of home ownership—and by that I mean purchase price plus interest on the mortgage, insurance, taxes, maintenance, and repairs—rose 47 percent. That's a big, big 15 percent difference. Only one out of twenty prospective home buyers can qualify financially for the average-priced home. A pretty sad overall picture. It's even sadder when you look at a specific case.

"We found the house we wanted at $67,000," Edward O'Brien, a twenty-eight-year-old research chemist, and the father of a four-year-old girl, told me. "Mary, my wife, works as a part-time librarian, and together we have a yearly income of about $27,000 before deductions. Not fabulous, but not bad. Our credit rating isn't just good, it's excellent. We pay our car loans promptly and ditto for our educational loans, and we've paid off a couple of personal loans which helped us to get started. So we expected no trouble when we went to the bank to talk mortgage.

"But," O'Brien went on, "the costs! We were babes in the woods—we had no idea what we were up against. The down payment alone was staggering. It was 20 percent of the cost of the house—$13,400! We both had worked our way through college; we were not what you would call rich kids. I only got my Ph.D. and my job two years ago, and we hadn't saved up much. You know, we had a baby and everything costs so much just to live. So that was the first splash of cold water in our faces.

"Next, the mortgage officer said to me, 'There's a fee you have to pay when you close the deal on your house, and that's 3 percent of the cost of the house, or $2,010.' Another $2,010! We'd have to put up not $13,400 but $15,410!" The fee to which O'Brien referred is called an "origination fee," and, like points, it's a way bankers get around state restrictions on the interest they can charge on mortgages.

"Interest on the mortgage would be 16 percent. I knew that was high, because my parents had bought a house several years back and had paid only 10 percent. But it was just a number until the mortgage officer told me what it meant to us in dollars and cents. Monthly payments—principal and interest—would amount to $715. But I would have to add to that the monthly payments on property taxes and insurance, and that would make a grand total of $865. Mary and I figured that on our income after deductions, and taking off car payments and other debts we had to meet, we would have only about $350 a month left to live on. We couldn't afford a house—not on $27,000 gross income. The loan officer said, 'We wouldn't give you a mortgage for a $67,000 house unless your income was at least $41,500.'"

O'Brien said, "If prices of housing would only go down. And if they don't go down, I wish interest rates would go down. If they just went down to 10 percent the way they used to be, it would only cost me a total of $615 a month, and we could squeeze by for a little while. My income is bound to increase, and just as soon as our daughter gets old enough to go to school, Mary will get a full-time job. That's provided, of course, we could raise the cash for the down payment and the fee."

Which brings me to another point. Suppose you were in the O'Briens' situation, and you had the money for down payment and other cash disbursements you have to make when you buy a house (I'll fill you in on them when we discuss the closing). Would you buy now, or would you wait until prices and/or interest rates came tumbling down?

BERNARD MELTZER'S ADVICE
ON WHETHER TO BUY A HOUSE NOW OR LATER

House values will continue to climb. Interest rates will fluctuate, but the trend will be upward. If you've made up your mind to buy a house, the time to buy it is now.

This I realize is controversial advice, so in all fairness let me present the other side of the picture as it was presented to me by a member of the audience at one of my seminars. He said, "High interest rates—16 percent and over—could bring countless homeowners to the brink of bankruptcy because of exorbitant monthly payments. It's much cheaper to rent—about half the cost of owning a home. It makes sense to rent, invest your savings in high-yield money funds, and buy only when you can make a large down payment. That cuts the size of the mortgage and the size of the monthly payments to amounts most people can live with."

He explained that when buyers need smaller mortgages, rates will come down in order to attract more people to the mortgage market. "And so far as buying now because prices on homes are going up," he added, "they won't continue to go up faster than the rate of inflation. They'll level out neck-and-neck with the rate of inflation, so there will be no difference in real value between the house you buy today and the house you buy when you can *really* afford to buy it."

But if you don't take that advice, and you have your heart set on buying a house today, let's see what creative buying methods can do for you. Maybe one of the variations on the conventional mortgage discussed below will work.

Adjustable mortgages. To understand this newest form of mortgage, you must have a clear idea of how the conventional kind of mortgage works. A mortgage, as you already know, is a loan with your property as security. If you don't pay back the loan, you lose your property. That's known as a foreclosure. You pay your loan in equal monthly installments. Some of your payment goes to pay the interest and some goes to pay the principal, which is the amount of money you borrowed. This process is called "amortization." When all the principal is paid, the debt is said to be "amortized." Now, on a regular loan, the rate of interest is established at the beginning of the mortgage, and it doesn't change as long as the mortgage is in effect, which in some cases can be thirty-five years. Some homeowners today are still enjoying 8 percent mortgages which they took out years and years ago.

On an adjustable mortgage, the interest rate varies during the life of the loan. It can go higher; it can go lower. The rate is based on the national average mortgage rate as published monthly by the Federal Home Board. (Or it can be based on any of four other consumer economic indexes. If you would like more information on these monthly rates, write Federal Home Loan Bank of New York, Floor 103, 1 World Trade Center, New York, NY 10048.) The rate may be adjusted every five years, every year, every six months, or at whatever interval the bank determines. At some banks, even though the interest rate changes every six months, payments are fixed for thirty-six months. That means if the interest rate should rise during that three-year period, you would be paying off more interest and less principal; your equity would therefore grow slowly. The reverse would be the case should the interest rate drop during the three-year period. At other banks, rises in the interest rate mean a higher monthly payment and/or a longer repayment term, and just the opposite situation when decreases in the interest rate occur. And with increases in the rate, your overall debt increases; so instead of your indebtedness decreasing with each payment, it can increase. This is called negative amortization, and is a frightening prospect when you have an adjustable mortgage.

Adjustable loans in general guarantee that rates will not change more than 3 percent every three to five years. But a difference of even ¼ percent can make a difference of thousands of dollars in interest costs over the life of your mortgage. If you bet that interest rates will go down, you can win big. But if they go up, you can lose just as big. Over the long run—and that can be forty years—adjustable mortgages are a gamble.

But there are two advantages of adjustable mortgages. Most banks offer lower rates for adjustable mortgages than for fixed mortgages. The average difference is about 2 percentage points, and can go as high as 3. And the second advantage is that some adjustable mortgages run for forty years, so monthly payments are lower than for fixed mortgages of the same amount.

Now all that is mathematics, and as I've said before, you don't solve human problems with mathematics. When people come to me and say, "Adjustable mortgages are very new. They have their drawbacks and their advantages. What's right for me?" I ask a number of questions: "How old are you? What do you do for a living? How have you invested your money over the years? How long before retirement? What do you predict your income will be a few years from now? What's your tax bracket?" On the basis of these questions, I get to know people as human beings, and I answer them as a human being. Let me give you some examples.

I learn that one woman is unmarried, she's been a librarian for twenty-odd years, she has all her money in passbook accounts, and she's looking forward to retirement in three years. Do you think this woman would want to take risks? No way. I say to this woman, "A fixed mortgage is right for you."

On the other hand, take another woman: She's opened and closed a number of businesses, has made money and lost money, she's in her late thirties and isn't even thinking about retirement, and she's certain that her income is going to go up, up, up in the years ahead. Now here's a woman who's accustomed to taking risks; and should rates rise, her increased income will easily take care of it. I ask her about her income right now, and she answers, "Right now, it's not all that hot. I'd like to keep my monthly payments down." There's no question that this woman would be better off with an adjustable mortgage.

Now why do I ask, "What's your tax bracket?" Interest is tax-deductible. When somebody says to me, "I'm in the 50 percent tax bracket," I point out even if over five years the interest rate goes up 3 percentage points, Uncle Sam is picking up the tab for 1½ of those points. But again, I temper this mathematical formula with an understanding of the questioner's inclination to take risks. If he has no such inclination, I would advise against an adjustable mortgage no matter how favorable the mathematics seem.

I'd like to point out that the tax mathematics of *any* kind of mortgage favor you if you're in the higher tax brackets. Let's say you're in the 30 percent bracket, and the interest payment on your mortgage is $346.71 a month. Since interest is deductible from your federal tax, you save $104.01 (30 percent of $346.71); your true interest payment is only $242.70. But when your tax bracket goes up to 60 percent, you save $208.03 (60 percent of $346.71); your true interest payment is only $138.68! The higher your tax bracket, the lower the real cost of your mortgage.

I want to add this comment about older people. Some move to the Sunbelt and buy new homes (although most retirees just stay where they are). Their incomes will be fixed or even decline over the years. They may be tempted to consider an adjustable mortgage because of the lower interest rate, but they're in no position to take risks. A fixed mortgage would be much better. But again, not all older people are alike, and they too must consider what's best for them based on their own life situations.

Graduated payment mortgages. A young couple came to me and said, "I'm told I can get a mortgage with savings of $100 to $200 a month at first, which seems to us pretty wonderful. And then the payments increase each year for five years until they become like everybody else's. In five years, our income will catch up, so that's okay with us. Is there any catch to this kind of mortgage?" My answer goes like this: "If this is the only way you can pay for your new home, I agree with you that a graduated payment mortgage is, as you say, 'pretty wonderful.' But there's nothing for nothing in this world. After the first five-year period, you'll actually be paying *more* each month than a person with a fixed mortgage for the same amount. You'll be paying so much more over the course of the mortgage that you'll end up with total interest charges many thousands of dollars above the cost of an equivalent fixed mortgage."

Equity-sharing mortgages. Would you like to give up some of the equity in your home in order to get a cheap mortgage? Well, that's what a lot of people of all ages are doing in California. The story is this: You alone don't buy the house; you have a silent partner—the bank. If you have a conventional mortgage, any increase in your house's value is all yours—the bank just gets back the balance of the mortgage. If you have an equity-sharing mortgage, the bank participates in any increase in value, just as a co-owner would. What the bank loses in lower interest rates, it makes up in profits when the house is eventually sold. Giving up part ownership of a house goes against the grain of a lot of people, and except in California, equity-sharing mortgages have not caught on. But if interest rates continue to soar as prices of houses climb steadily higher, you may want to investigate this kind of mortgage when your local banks announce its availability.

Reverse annuity mortgages. This kind of mortgage is not a way of acquiring a house, but a way of holding on to a house in retirement when maintenance costs and taxes soar while your income remains fixed or actually declines. It's still in its experimental stage, but it works something like this: Provided your home is mortgage-free, a bank will buy your home *and permit you to continue to live in it rent-free.* The selling price comes to you in a lump sum or, if you like, in monthly installments. This reverse mortgage is paid off by the sale of your house after your death.

As I said, it's experimental; and I don't think it will catch on. Again, it's not mathematics that inspires my prediction, but consideration of people as human beings. Very few older people would want to give up their home. They would much rather scrimp to pay maintenance costs and taxes. They feel a sense of psychological security knowing it's theirs. And besides, they would much rather leave their home to their children and grandchildren than to have the bank take it after they die.

Seller mortgages. In a high-interest mortgage market, sellers are hurt as well as buyers. A house can go begging for a buyer. So some sellers take over the mortgage themselves. The advantage to the buyer is that the interest rates ordinarily will be lower than conventional mortgage rates. You might ask your broker if he knows of any house where you can get a seller mortgage. It's a form of creative buying that's not uncommon.

Rollover mortgages. These are mortgages which are renegotiated, or "rolled over," after a fixed period of years, usually five. You get a break if the interest rates are down at the time of rollover; but if they're up, there's nothing for you to do but extend the term of your loan or increase monthly payments. This is a plan that has had great success in Canada, but has not as yet proved popular with American banks.

What I've talked to you about are the six forms of creative buying that you're likely to come across when you're hunting for a way to buy a house. I've counted more than thirty-seven other forms of creative buying, but they're so complex and so severely restricted in their application by state and federal laws that I would have to write another 30,000 words just to make them useful to you. What I would suggest to you is as follows: If you can't take advantage of any of the six kinds of mortgages I've just discussed, have a friendly talk with your agent and say to her, "This is my situation—I have so-and-so much cash, I have such-and-such income," and so on, and say straight out, *"You* tell me how I can get a home." I believe that if you're dealing with an experienced agent, she'll find a way, and it may be one of those thirty-seven other ways. She might even invent a new one just for you.

• *Step 5: The closing.* This is when the deed of the property actually changes hands. At the closing you're there, and so is the seller, and the attorneys on both sides, and a representative of the bank or mortgage company. In some cases, the seller doesn't appear; he signs the deed in advance and leaves everything for his attorney to handle. In many cases the broker sits in. There's a lot of ceremony involved, because you're making the biggest purchase of your life, and it should be treated solemnly.

The closing is also a time when you come face to face with a lot of costs that you may not have even thought existed if this is your first house. You're going to have to come up with legal fees for your attorney, with the points the bank tacked on to increase its profits, with the cost of title insurance, with property taxes due between closing and the first regular mortgage payment, with mortgage interest due for the same period, with the appraiser's fee if you haven't paid it yet, and with the first year's homeowner's insurance. Currently these costs range from 2 percent to 5 percent of the selling price of the house. On a $70,000 house that could be as much as $3,500. So there's another large wad of money you have to come up with before the house is yours.

• *Step 6: The registration of the deed.* Here's something a lot of people buying a house for the first time don't know. When you're handed over the deed at closing, the house is not legally yours. The house doesn't become yours until the deed is registered at the County Clerk's Office. You can do the registration yourself if you want to. But you've hired a lawyer; let him do it.

WHAT'S BEST—A USED HOUSE OR A NEW ONE, A CO-OP, A CONDO, A RENTED HOUSE, OR A MOBILE HOME?

When people ask me a question like this, I usually answer, "It's wonderful to be living in a country where there are so many varieties of living quarters. When I was a small boy my entire family of six lived in a walk-up tenement flat without a bath or toilet in the apartment, and without hot water or any heat except from a wood stove in the kitchen. So the fact that we have so many kinds of housing to choose from seems like a miracle that can only happen here." Then I say, "Picking the home that's right for you is something you can't decide on just on the basis of money. You have to take into consideration what I call your life situation—how old you are, what you do for a living, the size of your family, and your own likes and dislikes. For example, if you like city life, unless you can afford a townhouse, you'll be thinking only of co-ops, condos, or a rented apartment. On the other hand, if you like country life—*real* country life, with a detached house far away from everybody—you probably won't even consider a new house unless you build it yourself, since most new houses these days are going up in developments." So my answer to the questions boils down to this:

BERNARD MELTZER'S ADVICE ON THE BEST KIND OF HOME FOR YOU

The best kind of home for you is not necessarily the least expensive one or the most expensive one. It's the one that makes you and your family happy.

Let me expand on that advice. Happiness doesn't come from the home itself. It also comes from where the home is located. That's extremely important. Many people move because their neighborhoods have become rundown and unsafe, and they want to live in a safe community which is alive and growing. Many people are happy only in a warm climate, only where taxes are lower, only where there are leisure facilities, and so on. *Where* you live is as important as the kind of house you live in. That's the reason I'm going to discuss *where* you live first, then I'll tell you everything you should know about the kinds of homes available to you. With all that information you'll be able to make up your own mind about the best dwelling place for you and your family.

29. THE RIGHT LOCALITY FOR YOU.

Some people live all their lives in the same home, and once that was the general pattern of life in these United States. But with improved transportation, especially the automobile, we became a nation of wanderers, picking up stakes and settling wherever the opportunities looked best. That's how we settled the frontiers, and that's how our country grew from coast to coast. Funny thing, nowadays before a banker grants you a loan he likes to know you've been at the same residence for a number of years; but in the past it was the people who were on the move who in the long run were better equipped to pay back their loans than the people who stayed behind. It's still true today. There's a great wave of intelligent, hard-working people sweeping down the nation from the depressed states of the Northeast and Midwest to the booming states of the Southwest. These people are looking for their homes elsewhere because of new economic opportunities. If that's your major motivation, then the sooner you make your move the better. But just be careful. Be sure the opportunities *do* exist. Let me tell you a story.

This couple told me that they moved to the Sunbelt not because they liked the heat, but because they had read there was a great boom in the industrial cities there. The husband had been a salesman in a Midwestern state, and the wife had been a schoolteacher part-time. They had two adolescent kids, a girl and a boy. What this couple did was as follows: They had only a very small bank account, but they did have a house which they had bought for $35,000 some years before, and which had grown in value to $65,000. They sold it, used some of the money to transport themselves to a big industrial city in the Sunbelt, rented an apartment, and invested the remainder of the money in a service business—actually a business for repairing automobile batteries and selling reconditioned ones. You might ask why, since neither the husband nor the wife knew anything about this kind of business. For one thing, they had a limited amount of capital, so beggars couldn't be choosers, as the saying goes. For another, they felt that in the booming Sunbelt any kind of business would turn into a gold mine. *They were wrong!* The combination of their own inexperience in the field and the fact that the city they chose to live in was not a boomtown resulted in bankruptcy.

BERNARD MELTZER'S ADVICE ON MOVING TO ANOTHER PART OF THE COUNTRY

Make sure that the image you have in your head of the place you're moving to is a true one.

Now, how can you be sure of that without actually going there, and living there for a while? You can't. So that's the first thing to do when you're thinking of making a big move. Go to the place you have in mind and rent a furnished apartment for at least a month, and then act as if you were living there permanently. Go shopping, read the newspapers, listen to the local radio, talk to people—that's so important, talking to people. They'll tell you what *they* know about living conditions, because they've lived there for years or all of their lives. Now you'll find out not only if there are opportunities for you, but also you'll know all about the cost of living; the shopping, medical, and cultural facilities; how the climate changes as the year progresses; whether the people will accept you or treat you like a stranger; whether there's a church of your denomination or a synagogue nearby, and so on.

Meltzerism:
You can never know a place by visiting it. You must live in it.

Now, it's going to take time to do this preliminary living, and it's going to take money. But when you make a move, you don't want to move again in a short time; you want to settle in. Every bit of time, every dollar you spend, will be worthwhile. If you find the place doesn't match the image in your mind, you'll have avoided making one of the major mistakes of your life. On the other hand, if after living in a place for a month you decide it has everything you want and need, go right ahead and find the right kind of home for you in that place.

30. BUYING A NEW HOUSE.

There are two kinds of new houses which you can buy. The first is the house that's built especially for you. The second is the house that's built as part of a development. Let's take them one by one.

• *The built-to-order house.*   To begin with, this kind of home which is built to your specifications is going to cost you far more than a used house or a development house of comparable size. It's also going to get you far more deeply involved in the details of getting the house in shape for occupancy, and those details start with the selection of the site. Do you know whether there's proper drainage; whether there's gas, electricity, and phone facilities; whether there's proper sewage disposal, and so on? If you ever needed expert advice, now's the time. You'll need all the experts you have to employ to buy a used house plus an architect and a contractor. The architect is your key expert. Among other things he'll help you with your selection of the site and help you avoid the pitfalls; he'll draw up sketches and show you how you can get most of the things you want at the price you're willing to pay; and he'll oversee the work of the contractor. If an architect is a member of the American Institute of Architects, he'll probably be reliable. He'll recommend a contractor; and if the contractor is a member of the National Association of Home Builders, the chances are he'll do a good job.

It's going to take time to build a house, and there are going to be a lot of headaches. Before you get into all that, ask yourself: "Do I want a house built just for me to satisfy my emotional needs?" and if the answer is yes, ask, "Can I afford it?" Remember, you cannot get a mortgage on a house that hasn't been built. What you can get is a construction loan while the house is being built; then, after it's completed, you can get a loan based on your equity in it, which will be large enough to cover your construction loan. The interest costs mount up. Work them out, and work out your monthly payments, with your mortgage counselor at the bank, then answer the question "Can I afford it?"

If the answer is yes, then by all means go ahead and build—provided you have the emotional makeup that will let you sail unruffled through all the storms of house building.

A question I'm frequently asked is this: "Suppose I build a house, and the architect inspects it and okays it, but after I move in, things start to go wrong. What can I do about it?" You can do something about it *before* you start to build, not after. And what you do is this: You don't deal with any contractor who doesn't provide you with a National Association of Home Builders' Home Owner's Warranty. That gives you protection for ten years against any defects caused by the contractor.

• *The development house.* Building your own house is like having a suit made to order. Buying a development house is like buying a suit made from a standard pattern, or buying a suit off the rack. For that very reason, it's much cheaper than building a house to your specifications. If the house in a development is already built, you'll have to take it as is. But if you're choosing from a model, you can work out certain modifications. This is the easy way to get a new house, but don't think that you can do even that without experts. Ask your broker's opinion of the development, for example; and certainly bring in your lawyer from the time you're asked to sign a binder. There's nothing wrong with a development house if you like to live in a development. But if you've never lived in a development before, it's a good idea to ask others who have what life is like there. Development living is a special kind of living, and it may not be to your taste. If it isn't, keep looking for a used house elsewhere that you feel you can be happy in.

31. BUYING A CONDOMINIUM.

Most people think of condominiums—condos—as apartments. Some are, but some are not. A condominium may be a cluster of houses, attached or unattached. But whether the condo is a house or an apartment, it's legally regarded as a house. That's because it's bought like a house; you go through all the six house-buying steps I've already discussed, including taking out a mortgage. Where it differs from a house is in the following respects.

Your purchase price doesn't include only your dwelling place; it also includes your share of the land and all the other property held in common by your fellow condo owners. Let's say your condo is an apartment. Then you own a part of the land, the building, and the recreational facilities, which may include a golf course, a swimming pool, and even a movie house. You not only have the advantage of owning a house (for example, values go up and you can borrow against your equity), but you have the advantage of enjoying all the other facilities which you certainly could not afford as a house owner. In addition, you don't have to fight termites or keep the lawn mowed or be burdened by most homeowner chores. The management of the condo does all those things for you.

I believe that condos represent the wave of the future. In my opinion, within ten years almost all desirable apartments in the big cities, especially New York, will be converted into condos. City and state laws govern how that conversion takes place, and those laws are changing daily. If you are renting now, and your landlord gives you notice of intent to convert into a condo, your best bet is to call your lawyer at once —and when I say lawyer, I mean real estate lawyer. But remember my rule in dealing with experts: Be ready to ask the right questions. So be prepared with a knowledge of the details of condo ownership (they're much too long and detailed and boring to be included in a general book such as this one) by writing the National Association of Home Builders and requesting a copy of its *Condominium Buyer's Guide*. The address is 15th and M Streets, Washington, DC 20005.

When condos come up for discussion, I'm frequently asked, "What are the drawbacks?" From my experience, I would say that there are *possible* drawbacks which must be considered on an individual basis. For example, I ask prospective condo buyers, "Do you swim or play tennis?" Many people, particularly older people, say no. Then I say, "Do you know the swimming pool has to be cleaned and the tennis courts have to be maintained? And who do you think is paying his share for that work? You." Another possible drawback is that you'll run into inefficient management and the cost of maintaining the entire condo will be higher than it should be. In addition to the purchase price, you have to pay your share of maintenance costs, and inefficient management can increase that burden, which normally is actually higher than rent for an equivalent apartment. And one more drawback: If your apartment house is converted to a condo, the chances are the property taxes will go up; and you'll be hurt because you pay taxes on a condo just as you pay taxes on a house. What I would do if I were you and you are contemplating buying a condo is as follows: If you're moving into a condo, ask other condo owners about management, maintenance and maintenance costs, and anything else you want to know before you go into a deal. If you're in an apartment house about to be converted into a condo, try to have your lawyer or your broker get you all the information he or she can about the condominium developer, then make up your mind about what you want to do.

Conversions, though, have this advantage no matter what drawbacks develop: They can definitely be sold for more than you paid for them. When you buy a condo which you formerly rented, you usually get a huge discount. Immediately you take possession, you can sell at the regular price, and make a very substantial profit. But remember, everything depends on your life situation. If you're a young couple working in the big city, no matter what profit you made, the deal wouldn't make sense, because unless you could move to an equivalent apartment and rent it, which you might not be able to do, you would have no place to live. In that case you would have to buy another condo which most likely would cost you as much as or more than you received from your condo's sale. On the other hand, if you're a retired couple, and you have no ties to your apartment, you could take the windfall, move out of the city and rent a house somewhere, and put the bulk of your profits to work for you in CDs or money funds.

32. BUYING A COOPERATIVE.

A co-op differs from a condo in this basic respect: You own the condo. You can sell, lease, mortgage, will, or do anything else you like with it within the rules set up for condo ownership. But when you "buy" a co-op, you're really buying a share in the corporation that owns the building. You can't dispose of your share at will; you have to get approval of the board of directors of the corporation. You even have to get their approval when you want to make an alteration in your apartment. A co-op is never a house; it is always an apartment.

Condos are all over the nation, but co-ops are based mainly in the Northeast, particularly in the New York metropolitan area. They are meant for city dwellers who want the type of luxury living with which a co-op is associated, and are unable to find that kind of living in a condo or in a rented apartment. Theoretically, maintenance charges, which you pay in addition to the purchase price of your share, should be lower, because each co-op owner is a "landlord" and has a part in management. But professionals are hired to run the building, and they can be unresponsive to your demands, resulting in higher maintenance costs than necessary. As a practical matter, most co-ops cost more for maintenance than you would have to pay for rent in an equivalent apartment. And so far as the purchase price is concerned, often you're required to put all of it up in cash. There are some banks, though, that finance co-ops; your broker will be able to tell you their names and all the details. Which is cheaper to buy—a co-op or a condo? That depends on the individual case. Some condos are more expensive than co-ops and some co-ops are more expensive than condos.

From a human standpoint, if you've ever owned a home, you would prefer a condo, because the whole idea of ownership continues. But if you've always rented, then you might more easily accept the idea of a co-op, which resembles a renting relationship with a degree of tenant participation.

33. RENTING A HOUSE.

Many people, particularly in the big cities of this nation, rent their houses all their lives. There are good reasons for doing so. When you rent you're likely to be asked to put up a deposit of one or two months' rent, repayable to you at the end of the lease. You earn interest on the deposit while it's in an escrow account. Contrast that to the situation when you buy a house: You have to put up around 20 percent of the cost. Another reason why many people prefer to rent is that in general rentals are cheaper than mortgage and maintenance payments. There's also a good deal of flexibility that goes with rentals. Leases are as short as one year, and seldom longer than three. You can get up and go without the trouble of selling your property. And then there's convenience. As a renter, *you* don't worry about repairs, heating, air conditioning, maintenance, and on and on. The building management does all that for you.

On the other hand, when you rent you don't own. You have no chance to build up equity in your house, no chance to make a profit when you sell your house. Also, as a renter you don't get the tax breaks that a homeowner gets. A homeowner can take off interest on his mortgage as well as real estate taxes from his federal income tax, and sometimes from his state and city taxes. A renter cannot deduct any of his rent, unless he uses a part of his home for business purposes. Also, I predict that in the years ahead, rent control will be phased out, and rents will go sky-high. If you can afford a home, it is certainly to your economic advantage to buy one. But—and once again we must consider the human factor—if you feel happier renting than buying, then rent.

34. BUYING A MOBILE HOME.

"I think a mobile home is a wonderful idea," a retiree said to me. "My wife and I can travel all over the country and see sights we never saw before. And all the time, we'll be in our own home." This man was a city dweller, and had never seen a mobile home—otherwise he wouldn't have talked that way. What *he* was thinking of was a trailer; a mobile home is far from mobile. Few can be towed by a car; almost all need special equipment to move them. I want to repeat this: A mobile home is not a trailer or a camper. It is really a home. But it's a compact one, averaging about 14 by 66 feet. A typical mobile home contains in that small space a living room, a kitchen, a bedroom, a bathroom, and closets. All appliances and equipment in a new mobile home are up-to-date. A mobile home makes *its* home in a mobile home park, which is just that—a landscaped community of mobile homes. In such a park, the mobile home is serviced with sewage, trash removal, snow removal, water, and other facilities, including recreational areas.

The big, big advantage of a mobile home is the low, low cost. The costs involved are as follows: about 16 percent of the value as a down payment, a twelve-year mortgage which includes a three-year insurance policy, land rental at the mobile park, and installation of the home at the park. All that comes to about half of what you would pay in monthly installments for an average normal home. And you can still get a mobile home for under $30,000, and some under $25,000. Mortgage companies and small finance companies will finance them, and you can get VA and FHA backing as well. Taxes, which vary from state to state, are also low. So don't be surprised when I tell you that 50 percent of all new homes are mobile homes.

Is a mobile home something *you* would be happy in? Joan Mainzer, a retiree, told me that she and her husband wouldn't live in any other kind of home. "It's very, very inexpensive," she said. "It's small and compact, so it's easy to clean. You ask any woman who has to take care of a house what *that* means. There's lots of people around me, and something is always happening. Life in a mobile park is always fun."

On the other hand, there are a number of facts about mobile homes which could turn you off. For one thing, whereas regular homes increase in value, mobile homes decrease in value, sometimes at the rate of up to 40 percent in a year. (The newest mobile homes, though, are so well made that although they don't go up in value, they don't go down either.) For another thing, mobile parks are crowded, and a dozen families may be living within a hundred feet of your home. If you can put up with that lack of privacy, and you can stand noise (many mobile parks are noisy), fine; but a lot of us can't. Also, mobile parks are regimented. You can't bring pets in unless approved by management, you can't have more than a certain number of children, you can't play your radio or hi-fi after ten at night, and so on.

Most mobile home parks are for over-sixties, and considering everything that's not surprising. If you're a retiree, and can put up with conditions in a mobile home, and your income is limited, a mobile home is something you should seriously consider. There are mobile home parks all over the country, and if you don't like one, you can always take your home to another (even though it's expensive to do so); and that's something you couldn't do if you were stuck with a regular home you didn't like for one reason or another. As a retiree, you have the freedom to move as you please, and with a mobile home you can take advantage of it (although few people do). You can find out where the parks are situated by consulting *Woodall's Mobile Home and Park Directory* at your public library. But not all mobile home owners are on in age. Many young families find this kind of home the answer—at least temporarily—to the high cost of housing.

Now you know the choices you have when you think about where you're going to live and what kind of a dwelling you're going to live in. It's up to you to choose. Just remember that making that choice does not depend solely on finance, although that's a big part of it, but on your life situation, and what kind of home will make you and your family happy at this juncture.

Meltzerism:
When you make the right decision today, you're making an investment in your future happiness.

Chapter 8

Buying Your Car

YOU CAN NEVER HAVE ENOUGH INFORMATION ON HOW TO BUY A CAR

The second most important purchase you make in your life is when you buy a car. Maybe you've already bought not just one car but many. Maybe you're just starting out, and you're looking around for your first car. But whether you're a beginner or an experienced car buyer, there's something you can always learn that will make you happier with the car you get. That's why I'm going to talk about the problems most of us have experienced with our cars. Some of those problems are how to choose the right car; where to shop for a new car or a used car; how to inspect a car before buying; how to figure the costs of a car—the *true* costs; whether to lease or buy; what to do about insurance; how to protect yourself in case you get a lemon; and how to finance your car.

And talking about financing, with the price of cars going through the ceiling, few of us could afford one without borrowing. Once again, the truth comes forth: borrowing in the '80s is something we can't do without if we are to live happily in the '80s. And because cars do cost so much, I would like to start out this section by asking *you* a question—

DO YOU REALLY NEED A CAR?

Most of you will answer, "Absolutely. I can't get to work without a car. My wife can't go shopping without a car. We can't get the kids to school without a car. We wouldn't be able to vacation inexpensively without a car. We couldn't go to movies or dinner out or to a football or baseball game without a car. What kind of question is that, 'Do I need *a* car?' We really need *two* cars, and as the kids grow up, we're going to need three or more."

But what about some of the big cities—particularly the older cities in the East and Midwest—where public transportation, although not very comfortable, is frequent and fast—do you need a car there? A New Yorker told me, "I never even learned how to drive. The subways are horrible and they're getting worse, but they're faster than most cars at most times of the day or night. When I look at the cost of cars, and the cost of parking and garages, I'm very glad I never learned to drive."

And how about retirees who don't get around as much as they used to do, particularly retirees who live in leisure villages—do they need a car? "Maybe not," one retiree told me, "I suppose I could always find transportation one way or another if we needed it, but cars have been part of my life ever since I learned to drive, and I would feel lost without one. But, tell you what we did—we didn't need two cars, so we got rid of one."

I would say to you, don't feel that you *have* to own a car. Evaluate your life situation, and make a wise decision. If you don't need a car, if you can be happy without a car—what a tremendous amount of money you'll save over the years. Think about it.

SELECTING THE RIGHT CAR FOR YOU

How many of us pick the wrong kind of car and live to regret it! A lot of us are influenced by slick ads, especially on TV, and make a car selection solely on an emotional basis. Now, emotion has a part—a strong part—in every purchase. But could you have bought a house—or built a house—just on your emotional responses? You needed an awful lot of know-how and a team of experts to help you place your emotional response in focus. You'll use experts when you buy a car as well —your mechanic, the loan officer at your bank, the specialists who write for car and consumer magazines. But for the most part, you're going to have to rely on yourself. To begin with, it will be entirely up to you to determine the kind of car you *need* as well as want.

35. THE FACTORS TO CONSIDER WHEN YOU SELECT THE KIND OF CAR YOU NEED.

You should consider all of the following:
• Gas mileage
• Driving comfort

- Styling
- Use for long or short distances
- Use on freeways, city streets, or country roads
- Use mainly for yourself or mainly with passengers

When you weigh those factors—some factors will have more weight in your mind than others—you'll be able to decide whether you want a full-size, a midsize, a compact, or a subcompact. Selecting the size of a car is not, as many people think, purely a price decision. There's no sense in buying a subcompact to save money when a full-size fills your practical and emotional needs. But price, of course, *is* a factor; and if you're sensible you won't put yourself into hock by buying a full-size when a compact is all you can manage on your income. On the other hand, if you have your heart and soul set on a full-size and your budget says okay only to a midsize, there's nothing wrong about making adjustments in your budget—taking something out of the entertainment item or the vacation item, for example—and buying a full-size. Problems are never solved mathematically—I've said this before and I'll say it again—problems are solved by just being yourself. Let me help you be yourself with this bit of advice—

**BERNARD MELTZER'S ADVICE ON
SELECTING THE SIZE CAR THAT'S
RIGHT FOR YOU**

Decide what size you want, then work out a way to afford it with your present income.

---

36. How to pick the right car in the size you've selected.

This is your next problem. I can help you solve that problem with a—

Meltzerism:
Look over all the facts before you leap to a decision.

What does that mean when you're selecting a car? Just this: Find out as much as you can about the different makes of cars in the size you selected. You can do that by reading car magazines and consumer magazines. Ask your librarian for them. Get the April and October issues especially, because they're packed with information. Also, talk to your friends, and let them tell you about their life experiences with their cars. That will mean much more than going over a lot of statistics and engineering data. If your friends rave about car A and tell you to stay away from car B, you're ahead of the game. Another thing you could do is talk to an auto mechanic. You don't know any? Your friends or family members who have cars probably do. Ask them for names. Go around, introduce yourself, and tell them you're thinking about buying car A, and what do they think about it? Then see how you feel about cars A, B, C, and so on by taking the time to go around to dealers and test-driving them. That will give you the "feel" of the car; it will tell you not only how comfortable you are behind the wheel, but how you and the car fit together psychologically. I said you have to know the facts before you leap to a decision; I meant the emotional facts as well as the physical ones.

Now you come to your next problem—

37. How to Decide about Options.

A few pages back I said to you, "Before you do anything about buying a car, ask yourself, 'Do I really need one?'" That advice goes double for an option. Many extras add little to your comfort or safety; and the more gadgets you have the more chances you have of something going wrong—extras can mean extra headaches. And they can run up costs. I think everybody knows what air conditioning can do to your fuel consumption. In New York, where the powers that be are keeping a close watch on the budget, they've discontinued air conditioning on almost all the buses and saved a mint. But if you want to buy comfort, and you can't do without air conditioning, pay the price. Again, it's what you want on one side of the scale and what you can afford on the other. If you want to tilt the scale in favor of what you want—which is the only way to tilt it—then do without something else. I know a mature woman who bought a car with a stereo tape player, even though she didn't like music when she drove (it made her nervous). She bought it because "My grandchildren like it." She made the right decision.

But keep this fact in mind: One car expert estimates that if you answer the question "Do I really need this option?" honestly, you can save 15 to 20 percent of the car's purchase price. That's a *lot* of money.

All right, now you've settled on the car you want, and the options you want to go with it. Your next problem is: "Where do I shop for it?" I'm going to help you solve that problem by dividing the answer into two parts. The first part deals with a new car, and the second part deals with a used car.

38. How to shop for a new car.

First I want to talk about brokers. What they are really are car-buying services. You don't have time to shop, so you hand it over to one of these brokers. There are two advantages. One. They don't handle just one make of car or a few makes as dealers do; they offer a wide selection of makes. And two, brokers are buy-wise; they are real experts when it comes to getting the right price, so you save money even though you have to pay the broker a fee.

Sounds great. But should you use a broker? Consider these facts. You may not have a chance to test-drive before you place your order. That's not so good. Also, if something goes wrong after you buy the car, the broker will say, "Don't come to me. I don't have any facilities for servicing it." And even though you have a warranty, that's not so good either. And finally, no broker has a showroom or car lot. They sell by ads in car magazines and automotive trade journals, or through your credit union, or your alumni association, or your veterans' group. There's a kind of coldness about the transaction, as if you were dealing with a computer. That's not good if you like person-to-person contact when you buy a big-money item. So there are risks in dealing with a broker. On the other hand, you do save money, and you do save time. If you are a person who is accustomed to taking risks, I say you'll probably feel comfortable dealing with a broker. If you like to play it safe and take no chance of being sorry, think twice about dealing with a broker. And if you're in the middle of those two extremes, ask your friends or relatives who've had experience with specific brokers for their stories; and then make up your mind about what you want to do.

If you don't use a broker, you'll be dropping in on a car dealer. And that's the way most of us buy our new cars. Don't just pick one dealer: shop around. A car is a standard product; you'll get the same product at dealer A, or dealer B, or dealers X, Y, and Z. But one dealer's price could be lower than that of any other. It pays to take the time and effort to find that lowest price, because, according to one car expert, you can save as much as 20 percent of the purchase price.

39. How to shop for a used car.

There are four ways to buy a used car, and I'll deal with them one by one.

• *Buying from a used-car dealer,* which is the way most of us buy a used car, has its problems, as every American knows. Before I would deal with a used-car dealer, I would ask around and get a consensus of opinions from friends and relatives who have dealt with him firsthand or heard about him second- or thirdhand. If his reputation is good, I'd deal. But shop around to more than one used-car dealer before you buy. Prices vary, and you can get an excellent buy if you know what you're doing. By that I mean—but let me tell you a story.

A young woman called me and said, "Dr. Meltzer, I have a problem with a used-car purchase, and I hope you can help me." "I'll try," I said. "Tell me what it's about." She said, "I found the car I wanted, but the price seemed so low I couldn't believe it. I said I'd like to talk it over with my husband, and the salesman said, 'All right, but I can't guarantee the car will still be here when you get back.' That worried me, too, because it was such a bargain, but I did want my husband to see the car before I bought it. We didn't get back until the next day. My husband saw the car, and he liked it, and he said to the salesman, 'What's the price?' and the salesman gave him a price that was about 60 percent higher than the one he had quoted me, and he wouldn't budge no matter what I said. Dr. Meltzer, what can I do?" I said, "Nothing. You just didn't know what you were doing. The next time you go shopping for a car, remember this. . . ." And what I told her is as follows.

When a used-car salesman quotes you a price, ask him, "Is this for everything?" He'll probably say, "No." Then ask him, "What else has to be included?" Then he'll tell you that he has to add on taxes, and the cost of optional equipment. Then ask him for the total price. When he gives it to you, say, "Are you sure? This is it, nothing else?" Then—and this is very important—ask him to give you that price in writing. That's to stop him from raising the price in case you come back a day or so later. But getting it in writing isn't enough. I know of a man who did everything I've told you to do up to now, who came back with the price in writing, and the salesman said, "You have to see the manager." When the manager came out, he glared at the salesman and said, "Fred, you know you had no right to do this," and he tore up the paper. "I'm the only one in this place who has the authority to fix a price," he said to the man who wanted to buy a car. So if a salesman gives you a price in writing, say to him, "I would like the manager or the owner to sign it." In that way, you'll know the price is fixed, and nobody will be playing games with you.

Another thing: Don't go shopping unless you have some idea in advance about what the make of car you're looking for is selling for. You can get started by looking up prices in the *Blue Book* or *Edmund's Used Car Prices*. Ask your public librarian for them. Then be prepared to haggle. You won't have the experience of the used-car salesman, but you will know what a fair price is, and if you stand your ground you can usually get your way.

• *Buying from a private seller* is okay if you know the person. But don't be ashamed to bargain and get the right price.

Meltzerism:
When it's a matter of business, the best relationship between friends is a business relationship.

If you don't know the person you're buying from—let's say you answered an ad in the paper—what you have to do is make sure the person who's selling it to you is the legal owner. In most states, you can do that easily by going to, or calling up, the nearest office of the State Department of Motor Vehicles. Just look in your White Pages for the information. There may be a slight service fee—$1 or so—and a form to fill out, but you will get the answer in a day or two.

Here's one hitch to that. Let's say the seller is still paying off on the car. In that case, the report from the Department of Motor Vehicles will come back stating that he does *not* own the car. Don't get upset. Legally—and I stress this—*legally* the car belongs to the finance company or bank or wherever he made the car loan. He has no right to sell you the car. But what you do in that case is as follows:

You and the seller go to, let's say, the bank that financed the car. You pay back the car loan in full, and you pay the seller the difference. At this point, the bank will sign over the ownership certificate, and the seller will countersign it. You'll also receive the ownership certificate plus the registration card. That card is your proof that license fees are up to date. Now you're officially the legal owner.

• *Buying from car rental companies.* Although the used cars offered for sale by these companies have seen a lot of wear and tear, and been driven by as many as a hundred people, they're in pretty good shape for two reasons. One, they're only nine to fifteen months old on the average. And two, they've been maintained excellently. It's a good idea to call up your local rent-a-car people and ask them where their used-car lots are located.

• *Buying from auctions.* Car rental companies get rid of the cars they can't sell at their used-car lots by auctioning them off. Taxi companies and other outfits that operate fleets of cars—municipal and state departments for example—also auction off the cars they're discarding. Most used cars put on the auction block have had several years of wear.

But you can get bargains if you're looking for them. Auctions which are open to the public are usually announced by ads in your local papers. When you're shopping for a used car, keep your eyes open for them.

But before you buy a used car from any source, you can eliminate the "lemon problem" in the following way.

40. GIVE A USED CAR A "MEDICAL" BEFORE YOU BUY.

You'll want to know the car is healthy. You may not be an experienced car mechanic, but you certainly can get the feel of the car by giving it a workout—in heavy city traffic, on hills, on bumpy roads, and so on. If it comes out of the obstacle course you set up for it in good shape, you know you possibly have a peach. Then, too, looks tell a lot. Look at the car from every angle—get under it, for example (that's a very important angle)—then get a general impression. But if you want to be really sure of the car, spend the $25 or so you have to pay a mechanic to "diagnose" the condition of the car. He's the one who will tell you whether the following important elements of the car are okay: the cooling and exhaust systems, the front-end alignment, the brake linings, the frame, and the cylinder compression. Where can you find a mechanic you can trust? Ask your friends and relatives. Their real-life experience will guide you.

WHAT'S THE BEST WAY TO FINANCE YOUR CAR?

You've now reached the stage on your route to buying a car where you've made the choice and you're happy with it. Now comes the biggest problem of them all—how you are going to finance it. Most car buyers, particularly first-time buyers, think there's only one way—have the dealer handle the financing for you. Not so. Actually, there are three general ways, and I'll talk to you about them. But before I do, I want to point out the things you should be taking into account when you go shopping for an auto loan. Knowing about them can save you a lot of money.

41. WHAT TO ASK WHEN YOU SHOP FOR A CAR LOAN.

You can get an auto loan through your dealer, at small loan companies, at automobile finance companies, at commercial banks, at savings banks, at some Savings and Loan Associations, and at credit unions. Wherever you go, ask these questions:

• *What's the down payment?* The answer usually is such-and-such a percent of the price of the car. Since you know the price, you do a little arithmetic and you come up with the answer. But the answer could very well be the wrong one. You have to ask another question: "Do you figure the percentage on the car's price alone, or do you include sales tax, and the fees for license and registration?" The usual answer is, "Yes, we include all those items." Now you have a realistic figure; and you can ask yourself, "Can I afford it?"

• *What's the repayment period?* A man called and said to me, "I want to repay in the smallest possible installments. What's wrong with that?" Nothing, if the smallest possible installments are the only payments you can handle. But let's look at just one set of figures. Let's say you're borrowing $1,000 at 24 percent (that's the rate some car dealers are charging as this book goes to press). If you pay it off in sixty months, you get the lowest possible monthly installment. The total interest over that sixty months is—now watch this—$726.08. But if you had repaid the loan in the largest possible installments, which would wipe out the loan in twelve months, your total interest charges would be only $134.72. By paying in the smallest possible installments, you have to pay up to $591.36 more for every $1,000 you borrow. On a $5,000 loan that amounts to a very painful $2,958.60.

The shorter the repayment period, the more the amount of each installment, but the less interest you pay. If you're out to save money, take the shortest repayment period you can get. Also, make the biggest down payment you can make comfortably. The amount of the loan will be less, and so will your total interest charges.

• *What's the APR?* Those initials stand for Annual Percentage Rate, and they give you a true indication of what you're paying for your loan. It's not, in most cases, the simple interest rate, because loans are repaid in various ways, and you need an electronic computer to figure out what rate you're really paying. But with the APR you don't. To state it very simply, APR is the *true* interest rate. Ask for it. When you're shopping for a loan bargain, pick the loan with the lowest APR.

• *What's the total finance cost?* You probably find it as hard to grasp the concept of APR as most people do; and frankly, unless you're an accountant or a mathematician, you really won't understand it. I threw in a subsection on APR because it's something you should know about, and you'll impress the lender when you inquire about it. It's also very useful when comparing the charges of one loan source and another. But for something you can grasp at once, ask instead, "What's the total finance cost?" That's what you'll be paying for a loan in dollars—and you can understand *that*. So, as far as I'm concerned, the answer to that question gives you the best guide to comparison shopping that I know of when it comes to taking out any kind of loan.

• *What's what about payments?*   You don't really ask that question, but a number of other questions that add up to meaning the same thing. One question is: "Are there charges for late payments, and how much?" It's easy to see how important that is to you. Suppose payments come due a few days before payday when your cash resources are low; you'd probably be afraid you'd be stuck for late payments every month. So ask, "Is it possible for me to choose my own due date?" It usually is, so you can pick a date on which you'll have no trouble meeting your payment. Another question is: "What happens if I decide to pay off before the end of the loan?" The finance company or bank may stick you with all or part of the interest anyway. If you think you'll be able to pay off the loan fast, that could be a serious consideration. Obviously, in that case you would prefer a loan arrangement without penalty for prepayment.

And one final question, which I'm putting into a separate paragraph because it's an important one: "Is credit life and disability insurance, or any other kind of insurance, included in the loan?" Two reasons for asking this. One, you can get insurance cheaper elsewhere. And two, once the premiums are on the loan, you're paying interest on them. So what it amounts to is you're paying more and you're paying more interest. Not a good deal.

42. FINANCING YOUR CAR LOAN YOURSELF.

As I've already said, most Americans find it convenient to turn the financing over to the dealer. Of the many people I've talked to about buying a car, almost all said their only interest in financing is: "What's the down payment? And what do I have to pay every month?" But, as I've just pointed out, that could lead to problems; and now comes another—

Meltzerism:
The time to solve problems is before *they happen.*

When you buy from a dealer, he'll give you a "credit sales contract," which is a fancy name for an installment contract, which has all sorts of built-in booby traps (we'll get to that later on). But the dealer is in no financial position to tie up his money for from thirty-six to forty-eight months when he sells you a new car, or for twenty-four to forty-eight months when he sells you a used car. So what he does is sell the contract to a finance company or a bank, which is why you don't make payments directly to the dealer but to the finance source he's sold your contract to. That's one reason why you're paying such high rates when you deal with a dealer; the bank gives him less than you pay, so he has to keep the cost up to be able to skim off a profit. Easily the worst place to finance your car loan is at the dealer's.

The best place, if you don't do it yourself, is at a credit union. Rates are lowest of any finance source, and if you do get in trouble concerning payments, you'll get friendly cooperation in making things work out without the threat of repossession. Now, that's the danger on a credit sales contract. You can avoid it, and save money, by financing the car purchase yourself. When I tell people this, I usually get the following response: "But Dr. Meltzer, where can I get that kind of dough?" And I answer, "Borrow it."

Remember, I took a lot of time telling you all the ways you can borrow money—particularly how to borrow money inexpensively. Now what you've learned can come in handy. Suppose I said to you right now, "Name me two ways you can beat the high cost of car loans." What would you come up with? You would say, "Passbook loans and insurance loans," right? Both are very, very easy to get, the interest rates are the lowest you can find, and you don't have to put up your car as collateral. If things go wrong, and you can't pay, the bank simply takes the money out of your account; and, as you know, you never have to pay back the insurance company if you don't want to.

BERNARD MELTZER'S ADVICE ON FINANCING YOUR CAR

The least expensive way to do it, and the safest way, should you be unable to pay cash, is to finance it yourself through either a passbook or an insurance loan.

HOW TO PROTECT YOURSELF AFTER YOU'VE BOUGHT A CAR

Every car owner lives with the prospect of mechanical failure or accidents. This is a built-in worry that you take on when you buy a car. I think we all know this when we buy one, and we also know that life is a series of give-and-take situations, and that we have to give something to get something. What we get from the car is something so wonderful that we tend to forget it. At no other time in history has the average person been able to move about with such great freedom and to see so much of his country. The car has broadened our minds, given us an insight into how other people live. It has also permitted us to live in suburban and country calm, far away from the hustle-bustle of the big cities to which many of us commute each day. Yes, we have to worry when we buy a car. But there's no free lunch, and that's the price we have to pay for the special advantages that the mobility of a car gives us.

However, you should not minimize the disadvantages that go along with a car. I'm not going to give you a lecture on driving safely. It goes without saying that you should; and I'm assuming that you are a safe driver. But things happen beyond your control—most accidents are caused by the other guy—and you must be prepared money-wise for them. Also, you could get a car with defects—whether it's new or used—and you certainly don't want to spend your own money to set them right. So far as defects are concerned, what you need is a warranty. So far as driving dangers are concerned, what you need is car insurance. Let's talk about both ways to protect yourself, insurance first.

43. WHAT YOU SHOULD KNOW ABOUT CAR INSURANCE.

Every state has its own laws governing car insurance. In certain states, there are "financial responsibility laws" which state that you must be able to pay for any damages you cause with your car—whether those damages are against another car, against any kind of property, or against people. The state then sets a minimum dollar amount for the insurance you must carry to be able to pay. In other states, there are "no-fault insurance acts." These state that you're paid by the insurance company even if the accident *was* your fault; and the same goes for the other guy. The advantage of no-fault insurance is this: You don't have to sue, and neither does the other guy, so the insurance company doesn't get involved in legal red tape, which happens to be one of the most expensive commodities in the world, and the savings are passed on to you in the form of lower premiums.

• *What coverage do you get on a policy?* The coverage is called "liability limits," and is usually given by three figures separated by slashes, like this: 15/30/5. That means the insurance company will pay up to $15,000—that's what the 15 stands for—when you injure one person; $30,000 to cover the injuries of all persons you hurt; and $5,000 for property damage. What happens when damages are greater than the amount of your policy? You have to pay them out of your own pocket.

I advise you strongly to buy more liability insurance than what's legally required. Additional liability insurance is quite cheap—much less per $1,000 than for the required amount. And if you need more convincing, just remember the following facts: Liability insurance also covers your legal expenses, and protects others when you permit them to drive your car. It also protects you when you drive somebody else's car with permission. Liability insurance—as much as your budget can stand—is a "must."

Consider other kinds of insurance as well. What happens if *you* are hit by a hit-and-run driver? You're out of luck unless you're insured for just that possibility. How about fire and theft? You want protection against that, don't you? If you're in a big city, you should think about protection against vandalism; if you're in a part of the country where flooding is not uncommon, you should have flood insurance, and so on. There are some policies that offer "comprehensive" coverage, and you should ask your insurance salesman just how comprehensive they are. The wise thing to do is to get as much coverage as you can afford, including collision coverage.

And that brings me to this point. There's an old joke. A car owner goes to the insurance agent and signs a comprehensive policy. He says to the insurance agent, "Now, will you please tell me all the things I'm covered for?" "Sure," says the insurance agent. "You're covered for everything except what happens to you." The point I'm making is this. Policies written in the old-fashioned legal way are as difficult to understand as if they had been written in ancient Greek. If you get such a policy, ask the agent to go over it clause by clause and explain it to you in plain English. Some states require the policy to be written in plain English; and if you're in such a state, don't sign anything until you've read the policy through. As I said before, look before you leap to a decision.

Sometimes somebody stops me and says, "Dr. Meltzer, thank you for giving me advice on how to protect myself with car insurance. But can you please tell me how I can afford it?" That's a good question, and here's my answer.

• *How to lower car insurance costs.* I want to begin by telling you that about 20 percent of every dollar you spend to keep your car going is spent for insurance. And I also want to tell you that insurance costs are growing, and have been growing, faster than the rate of inflation. So you have to do everything you can to pay as little as possible for all the coverage you need. How you do that is as follows:

Shop around.   Rates vary, and vary widely, from company to company. Also, when you're making your phone calls, ask this question: "Does your company use commissioned salespeople?" If they say yes, be on your guard. Salespeople earn from 10 to 20 percent of the sale, and that's tacked onto your premiums. Why pay for the services—if you can call them services—of salespeople when you have to buy insurance anyway?

Do some self-insuring.   What do I mean by that? All policies offer you a "deductible." This is the amount of damage which the insurance company won't pay for. In other words, if you have a deductible of $250 and the damage is $1,000, the insurance company will pay only $750. Look at that $250 as the amount you can afford to pay in case of an accident. That's the amount *you're* insuring your car for. The advantages are as follows: The higher the deductible, the less the premiums. So if you can self-insure your car for $1,000—which is to say, you're taking out a policy with a deductible of $1,000—you can cut your premiums by as much as 50 percent. And in case you have to pay off, everything over $100 is tax-deductible.

Take advantage of your age.   If you're young, inquire about reduced premiums for attending driver training courses, having a B or better average, attending school more than a hundred miles from home, registering your car in your family's name rather than your own, and getting your family in essence to underwrite the insurance with a "restricted" policy. If you're over sixty-five, you're entitled in some states to lower rates. Those over sixty-five do not as a rule travel extensively by driving, so you can get another premium reduction by driving less than 7,500 miles a year. Overall, in your retirement years you can look forward to about a 50 percent cheaper insurance premium.

Inquire about special discounts.   There are all kinds of them availble, but they're not shouted from the housetops. If you're a safe driver, if you're insuring more than one car, if you don't smoke or drink, if you commute by train, if you don't take your car into the city, if you garage your car rather than park it in the street, if your bumpers are approved, and a lot of other ifs could add up to substantial savings. Ask your agent about every possible way you can save money.

Now I've covered insurance with one exception, and that is "mechanical breakdown insurance." That's one type of protection that could help you when your warranty expires. I'll get to it just as soon as I've finished telling you about—

44. WHAT YOU SHOULD KNOW ABOUT YOUR WARRANTY.

What a warranty does is give you assurance that the manufacturer has delivered a car to you which is free of defects. If by some chance a defect does appear, the company will pay the costs of having it corrected. What a warranty doesn't state is that if the car's a lemon the manufacturer will replace it with another car or give you your money back. To people who come to me and say, "What recourse do I have if I get a lemon?" my only answer is, "Take full advantage of your warranty," because there's very little else you can do. What you should do is try your very best to avoid buying a lemon by following the advice I've already given you.

Also be warned in advance that a warranty does not cover tires or battery and some other parts of the car. Read your warranty before you buy a car and know exactly what protection it offers. And also get to know how long that protection will last. Most new-car warranties last for twelve months or 12,000 miles, whichever comes first. If you buy a used car, your warranty may last only one hour, although ninety days is the average. Also used-car warranties aren't as liberal as new-car warranties, and you may have to foot part of the repair bills.

So all in all, while warranties do protect you, they don't protect you enough. That's why some dealers offer you a *service contract* which covers many parts not covered by a warranty, especially the all-important parts that carry power from the engine to the wheels. These contracts run for twelve months or 12,000 miles for used cars, and for thirty-six months or 36,000 miles for new cars. You have to pay for a service contract, but it rounds out your warranty protection to a large extent, and it stays in operation after your warranty has expired. A good investment.

I sometimes hear a comment like this about service contracts: "I don't like the idea of locking myself in to dealing with the service people the dealer selects." It's a valid objection, if you've investigated them and found them not to be the kind of people you want to deal with. In that case you may want to take out *mechanical breakdown insurance,* which gives you the same kind of coverage as a service contract does, but permits you to use any mechanic or service outfit you like, and picks up the bills as agreed upon.

SHOULD YOU LEASE OR BUY?

In recent years many people have said to me, "Much as I need a car, the hassle of ownership is too much for me. Wouldn't it be simpler if I just leased a car?"

There was a time when leasing a car was considered only by doctors, lawyers, other professionals, and corporations, the reason being that with their large incomes they could use the cost as a tax deduction. But since leasing doesn't require much of a down payment, and since down payments on cars have soared and will continue to soar, leasing is being considered by more and more people as an alternative to buying. What do I think about leasing? Here's my answer—

BERNARD MELTZER'S ADVICE ON WHETHER TO LEASE OR BUY A CAR

There's no black-and-white answer to this problem. Leasing offers many advantages, so you may want to pay a little more to lease. But if you keep your car for five years or longer, it becomes so much cheaper to buy than to lease that it makes a lot of sense to buy.

Now let me tell you about—

45. THE ADVANTAGES OF LEASING.

I would say there are four big advantages.

1. You don't have to make a large down payment.   So the money that would have gone to the "down" can be used any other way you please. There's more money for the kids, for home repairs, for vacations, and—we'll be getting to this in the third part of this book—particularly, there will be more money for investment. Let's see what the down payment is.

In most cases it consists of the first and last month's payment in advance plus the first year's license and registration fees. Not bad. Not bad at all. That's a far cry from 25 percent of the value of the car. In this case, you might say, there's no real down payment. This *could* happen if your credit is good—but only if your credit is good. I don't want to belabor the point, but I told you before how important a good credit rating is.

If your credit is shaky, your down payment is going to be larger. What happens is this: The leasing company establishes what it calls the "cap cost," or the "capitalized cost," or the "original value" of the car. This is what the leasing company paid for the car, plus whatever options you want to add, plus a fee that the leasing company adds to cover its expenses and to give the company a profit. What the leasing company calls a down payment is a "capitalized cost reduction," or a "cash reduction of original value." In other words, the money you put up reduces the cap cost of the car. This reduced cost is what is used to calculate your monthly payments. You can get away without paying this lump-sum capitalized cost reduction—a real down payment—if your credit standing is fair. In that case, you pay it off in your monthly installments.

2. Monthly payments are less than total monthly expenses when you buy a car. With a maintenance clause in the leasing contract, you know that for the length of the lease (usually one to three years), you won't have to pay one penny more for your car except for gasoline and insurance. Yes, the cost of tires is included in your monthly payments, provided the maintenance clause is included. And the group insurance rate is lower, too.

3. You don't have to go through the hassle of buying a car. The leasing company does the buying for you—getting you the make and model you want, often at less than you could buy it for, so the cap cost is usually about the same as the cost of a car you would buy for yourself. You also probably get a better car than you could buy for yourself. That's because the car salesman is not really interested in getting you the best buy, or just the accessories you need and nothing else; what he's interested in is his commission. On the other hand, the lease salesman is buying a car that has to be sold eventually, so he's on the lookout for a car that will bring top market value a few years in the future.

With that in mind, the leasing company also wants to keep the car in first-rate shape. When you have a maintenance clause in the leasing contract, the leasing company will not only routinely service the car, but it will handle every malfunction, including major repairs. And if, despite all precautions, your car should break down, the leasing company will supply you with another.

4. Even though you can only afford to buy a Pinto, you can lease an Oldsmobile for the same monthly payments. In general, when you lease you can step up into the next highest car price. If it's prestige you're after, you can ride around in a Cadillac.

46. KINDS OF LEASES.

There are two kinds of leases, the closed-end and the open-end. Let's look at them one by one:

• *The closed-end lease* is sometimes called the walk-away lease because when the lease is over, you can walk away from it with no responsibilities whatsoever. It's more costly than the open-end lease.

• *The open-end lease* involves an element of gambling, and you can get hurt. Let me explain: When you see the lease, the leasing company estimates what the car should be worth at the end of the lease period. The dollar value that the company sets is known as the "residual" or "bring-back value." Now, if the actual bring-back value is less than the estimated bring-back value, you're stuck for the difference, or at least part of the difference. If, on the other hand, the bring-back value is greater than the estimated value, you can benefit from the gain in some way.

No matter what kind of lease you enter into, there are a lot of ifs, ands, and buts you should take into consideration. So read the lease, and if you can't understand the language, ask questions. And to be sure you get the right answers, deal with a reputable leasing company. You'll find one just the way I told you how to find a reputable car dealer.

Meltzerism:
A reputable leasing company will put you in the right *car for the* right *amount of time at the* right *price.*

In other words, should you decide to lease instead of buy, it's not Bernard Meltzer who'll be solving the actual problems of buying for you, it will be the *right* leasing company.

So that's that about buying or leasing a car. But before I sign off, I want to talk once again about the wonders of the automobile. An analysis of the 1980 census showed that the great population shift of the years 1970 to 1980 was to—guess where? To resort areas! That doesn't mean everybody was retiring. It meant that, one, people were moving to places of natural beauty and pleasant climate *even though these places were pretty far from where they worked;* and, two, employers were setting up their offices and plants outside of the city and near outdoor recreation areas. Now, without the car, the millions of Americans who moved during these years simply couldn't commute over long distances, and they couldn't get around in remote places where there was no mass transportation. It's almost everybody's dream to live along seashores, lakes, rivers, mountains, ski resorts, hunting preserves, or in picturesque towns and villages. Now you can, thanks to the car.

And I want to repeat, it's another wonderful American invention that brings the car within the financial reach of everybody—the credit system. Now let's talk about that system and how it can buy you virtually anything you want.

Chapter 9

Buying Anything

WHAT'S THE BEST WAY TO BUY—CASH OR CREDIT?

I'll start with another story. There's a restaurant I go to frequently, and I'm very friendly with the owner. I usually pay with a credit card. But not too long ago, a pickpocket stole my wallet in the Philadelphia railroad station, and I paid the lunch bill with cash. "Why do you do that, Dr. Meltzer?" the owner said. And before I had a chance to tell him what had happened to me, he said, "You of all people should know that I have to pay the credit card companies 14 percent for every check that's paid with a credit card. I can't add 14 percent only to the checks of credit card customers, so I add 14 percent to everybody's check. When you pay cash, Dr. Meltzer, you're cheating yourself—you're paying for the service of the credit card, but you're not getting that service." Of course I knew that, and I told him how my credit cards had been stolen, and I assured him that I would continue to use them once I received my replacements.

The point of that story is: The cost of almost everything you buy has been inflated by the credit card. You might as well use the cards and get the services you're paying for anyway.

But that's only one reason for using a credit card, and not the most important reason. Let's now look at—

47. THE ADVANTAGES OF A CREDIT CARD.

• *You can get the use of money for up to fifty-five days free of charge.* Every credit card has a billing date, which means just that—that's the date all your billings are taken off the computer and sent to you. You have twenty-five days from your billing date to make payment *without interest being charged*. Now suppose you make a purchase *on* your billing date; it won't appear on your bill until the next billing date, thirty days hence; so you have the use of free money for an additional thirty days, for a grand total of fifty-five "free money days." All that time *your* money is picking up interest at your bank. So here's a way to spend money and make money at the same time.

If you use your credit card one day after your billing date, you have twenty-nine days before billing; add that to the twenty-five days you have to pay, you get fifty-four free money days. If you use your credit card two days after your billing date, you get fifty-three free money days; three days after, fifty-two free money days, and so on. So to get the most free money days, make your purchases on your billing date or as soon after as you can.

Sometimes you can get more than fifty-five free money days when the place where you used your credit card takes its time about reporting the sale to the credit company's computer. You can also get more free money days when you use your card out of state or abroad, because it takes longer to process a sale. There have been some cases where the free money days added up to 170—nearly six months. But those cases are unusual.

Free money days are available only when the banks or credit card companies charge you no fee for the use of your card. If you charge, say, $1,000 a year, and the bank charges you a yearly fee of $15, you're paying 1.5 percent for your money even on the free money days. But that's a lot less than your money is earning in a deposit account or a money fund, so you're still ahead of the game.

Of course, if you don't pay at the end of the twenty-five-day free money period, you will have to pay an interest charge, which will be more than you could earn at a bank. But even then, the cost of the money is cheap. Look at it this way. Let's say you're paying 18 percent a month for your credit card purchases. If you had yanked your money out of an easy-access CD to pay for your purchase, the money would not only earn you nothing but would cost you 1 percent. If you left the money in your CD, and paid the credit card loan from your income, your money would be earning you, say, 16 percent. Add to that the 1 percent you would have lost, and you get 17 percent. Subtract that from the 18 percent you're paying, and you get 1 percent—and that's the *true* cost of your credit card interest!

The same benefit accrues to you when you draw cash with your credit card. Provided you have money in a CD, the cost of your credit card loan is infinitesimal. But be warned of one thing: When you draw cash there are no free days. Your interest begins from the moment the teller hands over the money you requested.

• *You can take advantage of bargains.* Let's say you're short of cash, and the big department store in town has a sale on a $500 color TV for $350. Use your credit card (or the store's charge card, which we'll talk about in a little while, get the free days; and even if you decide to pay off in, say, six months, your interest charge will come to only about $30, so you're way ahead of the game.

• *You can raise a substantial sum of money fast.* Let's say you have a credit card from Bank A with a credit line of $2,000, and a gold American Express card with a credit line of the same amount. If you have no balance on either account, you can raise $4,000. Now I'm going to tell you something about credit cards which could be as dangerous as holding a live hand grenade in your hand. But it could be a great help to you if you need a lot of money fast, and have the means to pay it back.

The idea is this: If you have a Visa or a MasterCard from Bank A, there's no reason why you can't get a Visa or a MasterCard from Bank B, and so on from Banks C, D, E, F, etc. You can get a bank card from any bank issuing the card, provided the bank is in your residential neighborhood or in the vicinity of where you work. Now if you're able to get ten cards—and there's no reason why you shouldn't be—and your credit ceiling is $2,000 on each card, you can raise as much as $20,000 with no questions asked.

• *You can avoid the pitfalls of the installment contract.* First, let me tell you about the installment contract. It's a way of buying appliances, furniture, and many of the good things in life. It's sometimes called a time-purchase agreement, and it's fairly easy to get because the merchandise you buy acts as collateral. The major pitfall of this kind of contract is that you don't own what you've bought until the last cent has been paid. Suppose you can't pay off? I'll tell you a story.

An elderly woman stopped me and said, "I bought a hi-fi and a color TV on the installment plan. I paid off the monthly installments faithfully up to a point, but then I got sick and had to give up my job. I'm a widow and I don't have any funds in the bank that I would like to touch. So I couldn't pay." I said, "I know what happened. They told you they would take back your hi-fi and your TV." She said, "Yes. And that would be terrible. I don't know what I would do. I've paid almost all the money I owed them. Dr. Meltzer, can they do this to me?"

I had to tell her, "Yes, they *can* do it. But they really don't want to do it." Then I got in touch with the finance company, and arranged for her to make small payments, and everything was all right. But the point is this: Legally even if you only have one payment to make and you don't make it, the finance company could repossess whatever you bought. That cannot happen when you buy with a credit card. The moment you make a purchase, whatever you purchased belongs to you. If you get in trouble and find it hard to pay, the bank or credit card company cannot threaten you with repossession.

"But if I buy with a credit card, and what I buy is mine," I'm often asked, "what happens if I get a lemon, since I'm no longer dealing with the company I bought it from, I'm dealing with the bank?" Not too long ago, you would have had no recourse. But under the Fair Credit Billing Act which was passed in 1975, you can do two things, provided the item you bought was valued at over $50 and you made the purchase either in your home state or within a hundred miles of where you live. One, you can make a request in writing that you would like a refund or an exchange, or would like to have what's wrong with the item corrected. Second, you can send a copy of your letter to the bank. The moment the bank receives the copy, it's forbidden by the Fair Credit Billing Act to hurt your credit standing in any way should you decide not to pay for the item. What happens in cases like this, as a practical matter, is that the bank gets in touch with the company that sold you the item and works out some sort of deal that satisfies everybody.

Another question I'm often asked goes something like this: "I bought a typewriter on the installment plan. I still have a lot of installments to go, but I no longer have any use for it. My friend says he'll give me $100 for it. Can I sell it?" You could sell it, but you could get yourself in a lot of hot water in case you didn't pay up. Legally, you have no right to sell it, because it isn't yours; it's the finance company's. On the other hand, if you had bought the typewriter with a credit card, the moment the card is accepted, the typewriter becomes yours and you can do anything you want with it. You can sell it, pawn it, or give it away.

Credit card interest is usually many percentage points lower than installment credit interest. I would say buying with a credit card is much better for you than buying with an installment loan.

• *You can get discounts with your credit card when you offer to pay cash.* That comes about from the fact that the company which accepts the credit card has to pay the credit card company or bank 8 to 14 percent of the selling price. What you can say is, "Look, here's my credit card, and I intend to use it. But I'll pay in cash if you give me a 5 percent discount." Well, 5 percent is less than 8 to 14 percent, so some owners and store managers will agree. Issuers of credit cards hate this practice, so for a long time they would withdraw their credit card account from any company that offered discounts for cash. Now federal and state laws forbid the card issuers to do that; and merchants, restaurant owners, and so forth can give disconuts for cash without fear of reprisal from the card issuers. In practice, though, few of them do give discounts. But with prices continuing to go through the roof, it could be a good sales gimmick. I can see the ad headline now: *Bring in your credit card and get a 5 percent discount on anything!*

• *You can avoid the expense of travelers' checks.* Travelers' checks cost about 1 to 2 percent of their value. (Barclay's travelers' checks are free, but that's the exception.) You buy safety with travelers' checks, but you get the same kind of safety with credit cards, which are now accepted all over the world for almost anything. And remember, you can draw cash in the currency of the country you're in with credit cards.

• *You can keep accurate records for tax purposes.* It's awkward to pay cash and ask for receipts. As a matter of fact, in expensive restaurants waiters look down their nose at anybody who does that. But with a credit card purchase, you get a receipt automatically, plus a statement from the credit card issuer.

• *You can order by mail without having to tap your cash.* Formerly, as every mail-order buyer knows, the ads read, "Please send check or money order with order." Nowadays, you can order almost anything by mail just by giving your credit card number and the date of expiration. Instead of drawing on your cash, you can let it grow interest for you in your deposit account. Service is faster, too, because the mail-order merchandiser doesn't have to wait until your check clears, which in the case of an out-of-town supplier could take as long as a week.

• *You have an excellent source of identification.* Ask any traveler and he'll tell you that you simply can't register for a hotel without a credit card. Also, you can't rent a car without a credit card. Your credit card is really a passport which tells people you're you whenever you need identification. Actually, it's not an identification in the sense that a passport is a identification, but people have begun to accept it as more valid than a passport. Just try to register in an American hotel on the basis of an American passport, and the clerk will say to you, "You'll have to see the credit manager."

• *You can get discounts with some single-purpose cards.* What are they? They're cards issued by car-rental companies, airlines, motel chains, department stores, and so on. For the most part they're meant to be used for a single purpose—to buy in the places that issue the cards.

This is not always true. An airline card may allow you to charge at a motel chain, and vice versa. Many of these single-purpose card issuers offer discounts to their card holders, plus other special services such as express car rentals. The department-store card is a boon to those who want to return goods without a hassle and without worrying about refunds or credit slips. Also, almost every person who buys in a department store tells me he or she gets better service with a charge plate than when they pay with cash. T&E cards, in addition to offering discounts to corporate users, also offer free travel insurance under certain conditions, as well as standard traveler's insurance and emergency check-cashing facilities.

48. WHAT TO DO WHEN YOU LOSE A CREDIT CARD.

Before I get into that, I'd like to say that you should think of your credit cards as very valuable assets. Should you lose them, somebody could use them. Your liability is limited to $50 a card, but that's still $50. Take good care of your cards. I'm going to give you—
• *Six simple ways to keep your credit cards safe.*
1. Carry them in a see-through wallet so you know they're there all the time. Check your wallet several times during the day.
2. At home, keep your wallet out of reach and out of sight of *all* visitors. People are known to have sticky fingers.
3. When you're not using your cards for an extended period, keep them in a locked drawer, a strongbox, or a wall safe if you have one.
4. Minimize risks on trips by carrying as few cards as necessary. Before you retire, put them in the hotel safe. Some hotels provide a locked desk in your room. Take advantage of it.
5. When the entire family's away together on a trip, deposit the cards you're not taking with you in a bank safe deposit box.
6. Never keep your cards in the glove compartment of your car, and never, never in your luggage.
But in spite of all your precautions, your cards can be stolen. Mine were, as I told you, in the Philadelphia railroad station, and I never missed them until I got to New York. The thief was an expert. He removed my wallet, took out my cards, and returned my wallet to my pocket, and I never knew it. The first thing I did when I got to my office in New York was to call every card issuer. I gave them my name and the numbers of the cards, which I had on a sheet of paper in my desk, and I didn't have a thing to worry about unless the thief did some spending before I called. As it happened, he didn't. But the next day he

tried to use one of my cards. The clerk checked the number and saw it was on the hot list. He said to the thief, "Will you wait a minute, sir, while I get the manager's okay?" Then he went to the telephone and called the police. They came, and the thief was caught.

I said I called *every* card issuer. That proves I'm human and I goof up like everybody else—because there's an easier way to notify card issuers when you've lost your cards: Buy credit card insurance. You list all your cards with the insurance company, and in the event your cards are lost, you just make one call—to the insurance company—and the company will make all the other calls for you. The company also arranges for rapid replacement of your cards. One company goes even further. Should you lose your cards, your money, and your transportation tickets when you're out of town, the company will give you $100 in cash plus tickets to get you home. For further information on credit card insurance, write American Express, P.O. Box 765, Great Neck, NY 11025, or Credit Card Service Bureau of America, P.O. Box 1322, Alexandria, VA 22313. Credit card insurance is *cheap!*

BERNARD MELTZER'S ADVICE ON WHETHER TO PAY WITH CASH OR USE A CREDIT CARD

When you have a choice, unless you can get a discount by paying with cash, use your credit card.

This is not a consumerism book. If it were I'd go on at length and tell you how to shop for food, and for clothes, and for furniture, and for hospitalization, and so on. But this is a book about the wisest way to handle your personal finances, including the wisest way to buy anything. And you've seen—especially in buying the two most important items in your life, your home and your car—that the wisest way to buy anything, with some exceptions, is with credit. You can get everything—or almost everything—you want that way, and you'll save money.

The money you save helps build your excess supply of cash. What are you going to do with it? That's one of the big problems faced by any individual or family. Let me help you solve that problem in Part III by giving you my advice on how to invest, using your surplus money and borrowing as well.

PART III

Solving Your Investment Problems: How to Make the Safest, Most Profitable Investments—Using Borrowed Money (and Your Own)

Chapter 10

Solving the Inflation Problem

By this time you're getting a picture of what life is like in the '80s in the U.S.A. Ours is a society based on credit. That's one side of the picture. The other side is that it's a society based on inflation. Like it or not, inflation is a way of life. But is it a necessary evil? It has been in the past, when, for example, it wiped out the Weimar Republic in Germany and paved the way to Hitler. But the worst inflation in the world today is in Israel—more than 160 percent a year—and yet Israel is a strong, prospering country. How do you account for it? They have a built-in system by which as the prices go up so do wages and so do interest rates on savings. Changes in prices and interest rates are made from month to month. So if you're an Israeli, your finances always run neck and neck with inflation, and inflation doesn't bother you.

What causes inflation? Don't ask economists. Somebody once called economics "the dismal science." Scientists in fields such as physics, chemistry, and astronomy don't think economics is a science at all. When we wanted to go to the moon, we got a team of scientists together, and they decided there was only one way to go, and—zoom!—off we went. Get ten economists together and ask them the way to do anything, and you'll get twenty different answers. But you can figure out what inflation is all about if you use your common sense.

Just consider every item produced in this country as making one big pie. Let's say there are a billion items in the pie, and, just to make things simple, let's say all the items are the same price, $1. So there's a billion dollars ($1,000,000,000) in the pie. Following me? Okay.

Now let's say the government borrows a hundred million dollars ($100,000,000)—which is known as deficit spending. The pie is now worth 1.1 billion dollars ($1,000,000,000 plus $100,000,000). The cost of each item in the pie is figured by dividing the total value of the pie, 1.1 billion dollars, by the number of items in the pie, 1 billion. The answer is $1.10. So prices have gone up, and the rate of inflation is 10 percent. Simple, isn't it, when you use common sense.

Now watch this. Let's suppose productivity goes down; instead of 1 billion items in the pie, there are only 900,000,000 (.9 billion). To get the price of one item, divide $1.1 billion by .9 billion, and you get $1.22. That's the new price hike; and inflation is now 22 percent.

What causes inflation? You can now figure it out for yourself: government deficit spending and lower productivity. Put a stop to government deficit spending (which means getting rid of Keynesian economics), and increase productivity (which means getting back to good old-fashioned American work ethics), and inflation will be a thing of the past.

Will it happen? I hope so. But we can't live on hopes. Inflation is a part of our world, and I predict it will be a part of our world throughout the '80s at least, and we've got to learn to live with it. Inflation is the biggest problem each of us faces today so far as money is concerned. It terrifies a lot of us—especially people on fixed income. But it should hold no terrors for you. As a matter of fact, you can take advantage of it in two ways, and beat it in a third.

You take advantage of it, one, by borrowing, then repaying with inflation dollars, dollars that are worth less—you know that already—and, two, by investing your borrowed money, making a profit, and paying back your debt with inflation dollars, so you gain two ways. You can beat inflation by making investments that bring in returns higher than the percentage of inflation. If inflation is 10 percent, and you earn 15 percent—which is not hard to do at all—you're well ahead of the game.

You know all about borrowing, and how to use credit when you buy, so you've already solved part of the inflation problem. In this section, I'm going to show you how to solve the other parts: using credit to invest, and making the most profitable investments. And I'm going to do it as fast as I can and as simply as I can, just as I've done in the rest of this book. I made that point before but I'm emphasizing it now for two reasons. The first is that most people who give you financial advice use so many trade terms and assume you know so much that the advice, no matter how good it is, just can't be used because you don't understand it. And the second is, a lot of you are now very, very anxious to invest your money so you can beat inflation, rather than let it shrink in ordinary savings accounts; and you can't wait to wade through a whole lot of ifs, ands, and buts. I'm going to give you the general guidelines. The details you can work out with your broker, or banker, or even your gold coin dealer. But when you do talk with the people you're investing money with, you'll know what it's all about, and that will put you into the driver's seat every time.

Now, let's get going.

Chapter 11

Your First Investments: They Should Build Your Security Umbrella

Before we get into the subject of this chapter, let me give you some general advice.

BERNARD MELTZER'S ADVICE ON HOW TO INVEST

Anyone who gives the same advice to everyone on how to invest doesn't know what he's talking about. You have to invest according to the kind of person you are, and what life situation you're in.

Now I want to ask *you* a question. Would you say that a young unmarried man willing to take risks should invest in the same way as a retiree who has never taken a risk in his life? Your answer is right, he should not. There are all different kinds of people, and there are all different kinds of life situations. Toward the end of Part III, I'm going to tell you how people in some general categories of life situations should invest. I think everything I talked about in this book is leading up to that. Because that's the way—plus your job or your business—by which you will really get ahead. My parents, and all the other immigrants that came over with them, thought the streets of America were paved with gold. I will say this: The road to your future is paved with gold if you pick the road that's right for you. I don't mean real gold, of course; I mean profits with which you can do anything you please and enjoy life to the fullest.

But before I can tell you what kind of investments you—you, *as an individual*—should make, I want to introduce you to the kind of investments that are available to you. The first kind of investments I want to discuss are those that build your security umbrella.

49. HOW TO BUILD YOUR SECURITY UMBRELLA.

I don't think anybody should invest until he has enough money in the bank, free and clear, to last at least six months in case of loss of job, injury, or any other cause that stops or decreases income. That six-month money supply I call "your security umbrella." Fair enough?

Now, your security umbrella has to be *safe*. Where's the safest place for your savings? In a bank. That's because funds up to $100,000 are insured in case the bank closes its doors. Your security umbrella has to be *fluid*. That means you have to be able to draw out your money quickly when you need it. You can do that both with your checking account and with your savings accounts (although the bank could hold you up for a short time, but never does), and also with some other forms of deposit which I'll get to shortly. So a bank is a good place to build your security umbrella.

A great many people say to me these days, "But what about money market funds? I get a better return on my money." You sure do, sometimes 12 percentage points more. But they're not insured, even though I regard them as safe. Now here's where *you* as an individual come in. There's no risk when you invest your savings in a bank. There's a small risk when you invest in money funds. Do you want to take that risk? It's up to you. Here's what you can expect in the way of returns when you invest in banks and in money funds.

• *Savings accounts.* A lot of people don't think of putting money into a bank as an investment. It certainly is. You are actually lending money to the bank, and the bank is paying you interest on it. The amount of interest the bank can pay is determined by federal and state laws. As I write this page, the interest on checking and savings accounts is so low that they can't be considered as an investment by any serious investor. The return you get on your money is about half the inflation rate; so if you keep your dollars in a savings account, their value will shrink year after year after year. A retiree said to me, "That's a shocking thing to say, Dr. Meltzer. I was brought up to believe a savings account is the best place to keep my money." No, it's not—not anymore. Not at this moment as I'm writing. But it could change.

• *Savings and checking accounts of the future.* Between August 1,

1981, and August 1, 1985, the interest ceilings which the government has imposed on all deposits will be phased out. It won't be the turn of ordinary savings accounts—the kinds called "passbook" or "statement" savings—until August 1, 1985. At that time, I predict, the rates, which are now 5¼ percent in commercial banks and 5½ percent in thrift institutions, will double.

But what about the years between 1981 and 1985? The thrift institutions in this country—all the banks which depend primarily on the consumer for their funds—will *have* to raise their rates on ordinary savings to attract the money they need to operate profitably; and the government will have to permit them to do so *before* 1985. In October 1981, the National Credit Union Administration raised the ceilings on Federal credit union passbook accounts and interest-bearing checking accounts to 12 percent. But the chances are only about 40 percent of the nation's 2,500 credit unions will pay that amount.

Yet higher savings and checking account interest is the wave of the future for *all* kinds of banks. How much higher? That's anybody's guess. Should they go higher than the rate of inflation (the government reports that rate monthly, and almost every newspaper carries it), keep your money in one or the other of these accounts. If they don't, then try these other bank deposit accounts which give you safety and stability plus inflation-beating interest rates.

• *Easy-access CDs.*   Offered by some banks, these CDs—certificates of deposit—carry high interest rates, and they give you easy access to your money. The rates change from week to week because the interest you get is based on that week's interest on U.S. Treasury bills plus ¼ percent. U.S. Treasury bills, which are IOUs of the U.S. Treasury, are auctioned off each week and sold to the bidder who offers the highest price, which amounts to the lowest interest rate. However, when you invest in a CD, your interest rate remains fixed as of the day you bought it for the full term of the deposit, which on easy-access CDs is six months. On these CDs, interest rates are two to three times the rates paid on savings and checking accounts and sometimes higher.

Here's how an easy-access CD works at one commercial bank: By regulation, you must deposit at least $10,000. The easy-access privilege permits you to withdraw up to $7,000, and checks are issued to you for that purpose. Each check must be for a minimum of $500. The bank charges you 1 percent per year for every dollar you withdraw, so the more money you withdraw, the less interest you earn. Nevertheless, even if you withdraw the full $7,000, you'll still be earning about twice what a savings account or checking account would pay. You can even withdraw the final $3,000 if you like, but then the penalty becomes severe—usually about three months' interest—so if you do, you're not much better off than if you had put your money into a checking or savings account.

At one savings bank, no checks are issued, but access to your money is easy because you can borrow up to 80 percent of your deposit at 1 percent above the rate you're earning. Whether you withdraw by borrowing or by writing a check, the result is the same—the greater the amount you withdraw, the lower your interest. But in both cases, even if you withdraw the maximum permissible, you'll still be ahead of inflation.

At seminars which I conduct, I'm usually asked, "But Dr. Meltzer, I don't have $10,000 to put up. What shall I do?" You can still get a CD at a commercial bank. What happens is as follows: Bring in as little as $3,000, and the bank will lend you the other $7,000 to get started. The cost is 1 percent a year. You can't draw on the $7,000. But if you deposit $3,500 or more, you can withdraw by writing checks of $500 or more, provided you leave $3,000 in the account for the full six months.

On easy-access CDs, as on all CDs, all your deposit plus interest is yours on maturity date—that's the date when your six months are up. There's one exception to that rule: Some banks pay interest monthly or quarterly. On the whole, easy-access CDs are good sound investments. And they're a marvelous way to build your security umbrella by borrowing even when you don't have the $10,000 to put up.

• *All Savers* are one-year CDs which offer a phenomenal tax advantage. They're part of the new tax program, and are designed to bring around $250 billion into the nation's financial institutions, which are badly in need of it. What's this infusion of greenbacks supposed to do? The money is supposed to be loaned out, and that could stimulate new business activity, and more productivity. Good! That could help shrink the ranks of the unemployed and help curb inflation. Some of the money—actually, a good part—is supposed to go into mortgages with interest rates we could all live with. Very good! If it works out, that will spur the construction industry, which has been a pretty sick industry in recent years. To my mind, these All Savers make good common sense, and my hat's off to the team in the Administration that thought them up. I don't know if all the hopes for the All Savers will bear fruit—they just might not; when a nation's economics is concerned, we can't predict, we can only guess and hope—but I'm rooting for them.

Let me tell you how the All Savers work: The interest rate is fixed at 70 percent of the rate of one-year U.S. Treasury Bills in the week preceding the sale of the All Saver. Treasury Bills are U.S. Government IOUs which go up for auction every week, and the interest rate is established by the bidder who offers the highest price, which works out to the lowest interest rate. So interest rates fluctuate from week to week. However, when you buy an All Saver, the interest rate *you* get is fixed for a full year. Say a Treasury Bill last week was auctioned off at 15 percent interest. Should you buy an All Saver today you would get 70 percent of 15 percent, or 10.5 percent, for a full year. I predict average interest will be about 12 percent.

"So what's the big deal about getting 10.5 and 12 percent?" you might ask, when easy-access CDs and money funds pay more. The big deal is this. You can deduct up to $1,000 of your interest from federal taxes (and from some state and city taxes, too), and up to $2,000 if you file a joint return. Now bear with me while I go through some arithmetic, and I'll show you why that tax deduction is such a big deal.

Say you buy a regular $10,000 six-month CD—not an All Saver—at 15 percent. You earn simple interest, so at the end of six months you can cash in your certificate and come up with a profit of $750. Let's say you're in the 50 percent federal tax bracket. Half of your profit goes to Uncle Sam, and you're left with only $375. But say you buy an All Saver at 10.5 percent. At the end of the year, you would earn $1,050, and your six-month profit would come to $525, all of which is deductible from your federal tax. *You keep the whole $525.* Now compare: six months' profit on a regular CD, $375; six months' profit on an All Saver, $525. *You* tell *me* which is the better buy.

But I want to warn you, the mathematics are in your favor only if you're in the 30 percent tax bracket or in some higher tax bracket. I would not advise you to invest in an All Saver if you're filing an individual return and earning less than $18,000 a year. The same advice goes if you're filing a joint return and your total earnings are less than $36,000 a year.

What are the other drawbacks? *No easy access.* If you withdraw some or all of your money before the year is up, you lose the tax exemption. (There are some exceptions. Check when you invest.) *You may not buy with borrowed money.* If you do, you lose your tax exemption. In view of a major thesis of this book, which is that it's wise to borrow to invest, this is a big, big drawback. How the IRS is going to police this ruling, I don't know; but it's the law. *No ability to move your money into a higher-paying security.* You're effectively locked in for a full year, and you could be sitting around biting your fingernails as interest rates soar on other safe investments.

All Savers are available only from October 1, 1981, to December 31, 1982. The law permits All Savers to be sold in denominations of $500, so it's theoretically possible to buy a $500 certificate. But whether the banks will sell you one so small (they're not going to make much money on it) or whether you'll want to buy one so small (your tax gains will be piddling) remains to be seen. You can buy as many All Savers as you want during the fifteen-month period in which they're available, but you can't take more than the $1,000 deduction ($2,000 for joint returns) per year. Once you've used up your maximum deductions, you'll have to wait until 1985 to get a similar tax break. At that time, the new tax law will permit you to shelter up to 15 percent of income from interest.

All Savers are available from commercial and savings banks, savings and loan associations, and credit unions, but are not available from money funds.

• *Retail repros.* These are also called "repurchase agreements." This is a deal in which you really turn the tables on the bank—you lend the bank money and the bank has to put up collateral. The collateral is usually made up of U.S. Government or government agency securities owned by the bank; and when that's all the collateral is made up of, you can invest safely. How a retail repro works is as follows:

You lend the bank money for from eight to eighty-nine days, and the bank returns your money to you—that's the principal—at the end of the period, and mails you a check for interest the following day. Interest is high, about the same as for CDs. But unlike investing in CDs, you can deposit as little as $1,000, and you can withdraw your money any time without penalties.

As I said, if the collateral is good, this is a fine way to build your security umbrella. But—and here's the drawback—if the collateral is not good, then there's a big risk involved. Remember, these funds are *not* insured, and should a bank get into trouble, you could lose everything. Collateral of this type is rated from AAA to D, and one rating agency at the time this book is being written rates the collateral of most retail repros as C−, almost as low as you can get. What you have to do before you invest in this kind of fund is ask a bank officer for a prospectus. They're hard to read, so ask him, "Point out to me the kind of collateral that's backing up this deal." If you read that it's all U.S. Government or government agency securities, you can go ahead with the deal. Not otherwise.

BERNARD MELTZER'S ADVICE ON
HOW TO BUILD YOUR SECURITY UMBRELLA
AT BANKS

Building a security umbrella must be done without risk. The minimum risk is in easy-access CDs. They pay the highest insured rates, while giving you adequate access to your cash.

• *Investing in liquid-asset money funds.* A little bit of background. Often in my seminars, somebody gets up and says, "Dr. Meltzer, what about mutual funds?" And almost immediately after that somebody else gets up and says, "Dr. Meltzer, what *are* mutual funds?" I tell them that some companies go ahead and buy millions, sometimes billions, of dollars worth of stocks and bonds and other types of securities, and put them all into one big pile. The idea is, some investments may go down in value, and some may go up, but overall the value of the pie will be high, and over a period of time, will tend to go even higher. The companies hire financial experts who know what to buy. Each company sells shares in the pie. The pie is called a mutual fund.

Now, companies sometimes limit their securities to U.S. Government, bank, and big-corporation IOUs. These IOUs are *usually* short-term obligations of the government of the United States or its agencies; CDs worth $100,000 and more and bankers' acceptances from banks with assets of over $1 billion; and corporate commercial paper rated Prime-1 by Moody's or A-1 by Standard and Poor's. Don't let the strange terms confuse you; as I said, they're all IOUs of one form or another. Moody's and Standard and Poor's are agencies that rate securities, and Prime-1 and A-1 are top ratings. I say "usually" these securities are as gilt-edged as I described them. But they are not always so, so you must be careful. Be sure to read the prospectus, and if they are not as I described them, hesitate to put your money in that fund. At all events, companies which buy only money market instruments, which is what all these IOUs are called collectively, are called "money funds," or "money market funds."

On the average, money funds pay more than short-term CDs. The interest is also compounded daily. The interest on CDs is not compounded at all. Compound interest returns more money than noncompounded interest, which is called simple interest. The more often interest is compounded, the more returns it brings in. Interest compounded daily brings in more money, for example, than interest compounded weekly—and is the best way for you to earn interest. So that's another advantage a money fund has over a CD. Here are some others: You can invest in a money fund for as little as $2,500. And in liquid-asset money funds, you can draw out your money at any time without penalty, and checks are given you for that purpose.

When you invest in a money fund, you're actually buying a share in a mutual fund. The value of the share is usually set at $1, and should not go up or down; so when you put in $1, you get out $1 plus what the dollar earns for you. *That* amount varies depending on the total value of the pie, so what you earn on each $1 varies from week to week. Over a year, though, the earnings have been consistently the highest a small investor can get with safety. I'm for money funds, provided you go into them with your eyes wide open (so you can read the prospectus), and you're fully aware that there's a risk involved, even though it's a small one.

You can start to look into money funds by reading the ads, then writing or calling and asking for a prospectus. If you decide to go ahead, you can make your first investment, and all investments after that, by mail—and the whole procedure is quite simple. Money funds, when they incorporate the easy-access feature, are the chief rivals to short-term CDs, and justifiably so.

And those are the choices available to you when you're building your security umbrella. "But what about U.S. Savings Bonds?" I'm often asked, especially by older citizens who invested in them back when they were an excellent choice for the small investor. But their interest rates are now far behind the rate of inflation, and they are not recommended as an investment at all.

The next question I'm frequently asked is: "I've built up my security umbrella. If anything goes wrong I have at least six months' money to fall back on. My money is still building. I'm just an average person. Tell me, Dr. Meltzer, which investments are best for me?"

I'll have the answers for you in the next chapter.

Chapter 12

Investments to Beat Inflation Available to the Small Investor

50. THE BEST INVESTMENT: YOUR HOME.

The greatest number of pages of this book are devoted to your home, and a major reason for that is it's such a wonderful investment for these times. Conservatively, the value of your home goes up by about 2.5 percent a year over inflation values. So if inflation goes up by 10 percent, the value of your home goes up by 12.5 percent. I said I'm being conservative. In many parts of the country, it goes up about twice the rate of inflation. You can depend on the value of your home at least doubling in ten years, and possibly quadrupling. When you consider that you bought your home by borrowing, and you put up only 20 percent or less of the value of your home when you bought it, the return on your down payment is simply staggering. For most homes, all payments you made considered, your return per annum on the day you sell your house averages several times the rate of inflation during the time you owned your house.

There are skeptics who say, "That looks good on paper. But as the years go by, I don't see any profits; all I see is expenses." True. A house doesn't pay you interest. "And what's more," say these skeptics, "how do I know I can sell my house, let alone sell it at a very high price?" I say, as long as America exists, you'll be able to sell your house, provided you've bought it with care and kept it in good condition, and it's not in a neighborhood on the decline. And I say, real estate values have been climbing steadily, and they'll continue to climb. The drawback of not seeing monthly interest? Well, you're living in the house, aren't you?

You feel happy and very special because you are. Isn't that interest? And when you do sell, and you see all that money, you'll be very happy that it didn't come to you in dribs and drabs which you would have been likely to let slip through your fingers.

There are two tax advantages from owning a home as well. All taxes levied on your home are deductible from your federal tax, and at age fifty-five or over you get the tax break of a lifetime. You can sell your home for a profit of up to $150,000 and not have to pay Uncle Sam a cent; and you only pay tax on 25 percent of the money you receive over $150,000. Also, if you sell your home at any time in your life and buy a new one within two years, you get a tax deferment on the profits from the sale.

All in all, from the financial *and* the emotional standpoint, there is nothing like owning your own home.

Now I'd like to tell you about some other investments which are good for you.

51. LONG-TERM CDs.

They pay a few percentage points less than short-term CDs. You need at least $10,000 to make an investment, and your money is tied up many years (investigate what your bank has to offer), with severe penalties for early withdrawal. In some cases, withdrawal is not permitted at all.

But these kinds of CDs are being phased out, as government regulations make acquiring long-term CDs easier for the small investor and far more attractive in terms of interest rates. Since August 1, 1981, interest rates on thirty-month certificates have been pegged to those on thirty-month Treasury securities, which at the time this book went to press were about 14.5 percent. As of the same date, rate ceilings on deposits of four years maturity or more were eliminated. From August 1, 1981, to August 1, 1985, ceilings on deposits of between thirty months and four years are to be eliminated on a stagger system. There will be no ceilings on these kinds of deposits after August 1, 1985.

What long-term CD rates will be down the road is anybody's guess, but I predict they will be higher than the rate of inflation. As I write (September 1981), one bank is offering a sky-high interest rate about 1 to 2 points above the highest-paying money fund; and another bank is planning to offer a record-breaking 20 percent. The banks are attaching these interest rates to a forty-eight-month CD and a sixty-six-month CD respectively. The interest is calculated on a simple basis. I predict that the interest will be shortly calculated on a compound basis as the demand for your money becomes more urgent. Let me show you what that would mean to you. A $10,000 forty-eight-month CD which at maturity (end of the forty-eight months) brings in $17,200 at simple interest would bring in $19,387 if it were compounded just once a year. That's a difference of more than $2,000!

If you don't feel like tying up your money for several years, you could stay with your short-term CDs. I believe the rates will go up in the years ahead, and come close, or at times even equal or surpass, the new long-term rates. Keep your eyes open and take advantage of the forthcoming war between short-term and long-term CD rates.

• *Should you borrow to buy CDs?*   That's a question that comes up more and more. Certainly CDs are very attractive to people who see their money shrinking in savings accounts, and there is an exodus from savings accounts to CDs. Certainly 20 percent (if you can get it) is better than 5¼ percent. But if you're going to pay as high as 21 percent for a personal loan in a bank, you'll be losing money to borrow in order to buy a CD.

But there are other ways to look at the problem. If you can borrow for considerably less than the 20 percent (or whatever the highest interest you can earn), borrowing to get a CD should be something you should consider. Where can you get a loan at cheap interest rates? You know the answer because I've told you about it in the early pages of this book.

You can borrow on your life insurance at 4 to 8 percent and make up to 16 percent on the money when you invest in a long-term CD. There's no loss to your beneficiary, because the money is locked up in the CD and becomes part of the estate. A further advantage is that you don't have to pay back the insurance company anything but interest until the CD matures.

You can borrow on your savings account.   When I say this, there's always somebody who will ask, "Why can't I just withdraw from my savings account and put it into a CD? Isn't 20 percent better than 5½ percent?" I answer, "Yes. But how would you like to get the 20 percent and *still* earn the 5½ percent?" Then I explain that if you borrow from your savings account, the money you borrowed is still earning interest in the savings account, say 5½ percent, so you are collecting 25½ percent even though you may be paying something like 12 percent on the money you borrow.

BERNARD MELTZER'S ADVICE ON
BORROWING TO BUY CDs

Do it provided the percentage point spread between the interest you pay and the interest you get is greater than the rate of inflation.

"Does the same rule apply to investing in money funds?" I'm asked frequently. The answer is yes, provided you invest in the kinds of money funds that are safe. And I will say this: It's always right to borrow when you know the investment is safe and you follow my advice on borrowing. Let that be your guide to borrowing when you make any of my recommended investments.

> **Meltzerism:**
> *Borrowing can be profitable.*

Now let's get back to other investments to beat inflation.

52. MONEY FUNDS.

If you've used a money fund to build your security umbrella, there's no reason in the world why you shouldn't continue to do so to beat inflation after your security umbrella has been built.

53. ANNUITIES.

There are two new kinds: *single premium deferred annuities,* and *variable premium deferred annuities*. Both are designed to give you an income *after* retirement. If you want your profits now, and you don't want to tie up your money until your retirement years, you'll be tempted to skip over this section. Don't.

> **Meltzerism:**
> *The wise person begins to retire*
> *the moment he or she begins to work.*

Planning for your retirement is one of the most important acts of your life. You may have thirty years of life or more after retirement, and they could be the happiest years of your life. But they won't be if you're not financially secure. So let's take a look at annuities, keeping in mind that there are other ways to bring in money after sixty-five.

• *Single premium deferred annuities* take a large sum of money from you—a very large sum—and promise in return to pay you a "salary" after retirement on a regular basis for a certain number of years, or usually as long as you live. Naturally, you'll be paid interest, which is less than you'll get in a savings account; but extra interest is added on at the end of each year, which varies from year to year. The total interest has been averaging out about 2 points over the rate of inflation. The "deferred" feature of these annuities means that you don't have to pay taxes on your yearly profits until you retire. You will have to pay them then, but you will be in a much lower tax bracket, so the tax savings will be considerable. An annuity is also a solid asset when you want to borrow money. I haven't discussed this before with you because while, I would think, everybody reading this book has a savings or checknig account, relatively few of you have annuities. One last word about these annuities: Should you wish to withdraw your money, you can be hit with a whopping 5 percent penalty on the amount you withdraw.

Your "salary" is actually a repayment of your investment plus deferred interest. If you buy a lifetime annuity, rather than an annuity covering a fixed number of years, the amount of each payment is figured out so you'll never outlive the money in your annuity. You can buy single premium deferred annuities from insurance companies.

• *Variable premium deferred annuities.* These are very new, and they're run by money fund companies. How they work is as follows: You can start with just a few thousand dollars. The annuity is tied in to a money fund—with easy-access privileges. That means you can take your money out at any time without penalty. You can put in your money at any time as well. Money funds, as you know, pay high interest rates, several points higher than single premium annuities. The money you put in annually is tax-deductible. In this respect, this type of annuity resembles the IRA and Keogh Plans, which are also tax shelters. The "deferred" aspect is the same as in single premium annuities; when the money is withdrawn after retirement, you pay taxes on your interest for the first time. Of course, those taxes will be lower than in preretirement years.

• *What's better—single or variable?* From the mathematical viewpoint, variable. That's the advice every financial expert will give. But not me. The solution is human, not mathematical. What kind of a person are you? Are you willing to put up a great deal of money, and not see it again until retirement without paying a 5 percent penalty? Are you satisfied to see your money grow at about or just above the rate of inflation? Will you not be worried that inflation will spurt, and your annuity will be paying you less than the rate of inflation? If you answer all those questions yes, a single premium annuity could be for you. On the other hand, are you the kind of a person who will make deposits on a steady annual basis from now until the time to retire? Will you resist the temptation to withdraw funds? And are you interested in the highest interest you can get, provided it's always above the level of inflation? Answer all *those* questions yes, and the variable premium annuity could be just right for you.

You could borrow to get into a variable premium annuity, but it makes no sense to borrow to get into a single premium annuity.

When I talk about annuities, I'm always asked, "But what about the Keogh plan and the IRA?" All right, let's talk about them.

• *IRAs* (*Individual Retirement Accounts*) *and Keogh Plans* can be regarded as annuities, but their primary purpose is to act as tax shelters. Up to January 1, 1982, an IRA account was only for employees not covered by a pension plan. Under the new tax law, even though you have a pension plan, you're eligible. The Keogh Plan is for self-employed people. Let's take them one by one.

IRAs. You can take up to $2,000 of your income from wages or salaries and put it into one of these accounts, which are available at savings banks, brokerage firms, investment management companies, and insurance companies. If you have a spouse who doesn't work, you can set up a separate account for him or her, provided the total of both accounts is no more than $2,250, and the amount in the nonworking spouse's account is not less than $250.

Now the marvelous part about an IRA is that the money you deposit is tax-deductible, and the interest you earn is deferred until after retirement, when you'll be in a lower tax bracket. Without a tax bite, your money, which is compounded, grows pretty rapidly. At 12 percent—which is what you can currently expect in an IRA—your money doubles every six years. At the age of twenty-five, start saving $2,000 a year in an IRA, and by the time you're forty-five, your account is not worth $40,000 ($2,000 times twenty years) but $160,000! That's the magic of compound interest. Keep making those $2,000 investments until you're sixty-five, and you can start your retirement not with $80,000 ($2,000 times forty years), but with—I almost don't believe this myself —$1,700,000! It pays—really pays big—to start planning for your retirement when you're young.

"But, Dr. Meltzer," a young man said to me, "I only earn $10,000 a year before taxes. I'm married, and I have my first kid on the way. How can I put aside $2,000 a year?" "You can't," I answered. "But you don't have to put aside $2,000; you can put aside anything up to $2,000. Try to put something aside. It's a good habit to get into, and as the years pass and you earn more and more, put in more and more."

But in all fairness to that young man and lots of others like him, I want to say that the new tax laws, which govern the IRAs and Keoghs and other investments, were not made with lower-income people in mind. They benefit everybody directly to some degree, but they benefit the affluent more. In the long run that's supposed to be good for everybody—because the less taxes people who are well off pay, the more money will be available for investments, and more investments mean increased productivity, which in turn will bring down the rate of inflation and interest rates, and increase the number of jobs. That's the theory—and, I admit, I like it. I think it's going to work; it looks *that* good on paper. But paper isn't life, and so we'll just have to wait and see, and hope for the best. But to get back to my point: Unless you have a family income of at least $36,000 a year, don't expect to profit directly from the new tax laws.

Before I finish with IRAs, I'd like to tell you that you can also set up this kind of an account in the company you work for. No, not through your thrift plan—the kind of plan in which for every $1 you save your company puts up 50¢ or some such sum. That's not an IRA, and it cannot be converted to an IRA. But your company can set up an IRA plan based on your voluntary contributions, and with no matching deposits from your company. These company IRAs can be savings plans, pension plans, or profit-sharing plans.

Which is better for you—a company IRA savings plan or a company matching thrift plan? The mathematics are too complex to go into here, but my educated guess is that if a company matches your $1 with as little as 10¢, you're better off with a matching thrift plan than an IRA. There may be special cases where this is not true, so it would be wise to sit down with whoever is in charge of these plans at your company and work out which plan is of greater benefit to you.

Opening an IRA anyplace is simple. All you have to do is put money into almost any investment—a bank account, for example, or a money fund, or a company fund—and fill out a form which states you've set up an IRA account. That's all there is to it. But you cannot set up an IRA account in collectibles (gems, stamps, coins, art, and so on), in insurance, or in any investment paid for with borrowed money.

Keoghs.   They operate for the self-employed much as the IRAs operate for employees. You can invest up to $15,000 a year in a Keogh. You can also put up to $2,000 more into an IRA, for a total of $17,000 which is exempt from federal tax. But you can't put in more than 15 percent of your income.

Is an IRA or Keogh right for you?   Both IRA and Keogh are excellent tax shelters. But before you plunge in, take these facts into consideration. Your money is locked in, and cannot be withdrawn until you're at least 59½ years old without a penalty. The penalty is severe—10 percent of the sum taken out early plus tax on that sum. Let's say you take out $10,000 and you're in the 30 percent tax bracket. You get hit by a 10 percent penalty which reduces the $10,000 to $9,000. Then Uncle Sam takes 30 percent of the $10,000—$3,000—so you end up with only $6,000 out of *your* $10,000. See what I mean when I said the penalty is severe?

Another drawback: You can't put any money into your IRA or Keogh after age 70½, and you must start drawing out your money at that time. How fast? The government figures out how long you're going to live based on insurance-company statistics, and makes up a schedule which permits you to draw out your investment gradually until the end of your lifespan. You could draw it out faster, of course.

What interest do you get on your IRA or Keogh? As much as your investment pays. Mutual funds, especially money funds, are your best bet in this respect, although they do sometimes hit you with yearly custodial fees, as well as commissions and management fees. But even with all costs deducted, the rate of return will be higher than the rate of inflation.

You could also ask your bank to set up an IRA for you based on investments in stocks, bonds, and so on. The returns on your investment are subject to the ups and downs of the stock market, but you have a chance of staying ahead of inflation. You also have a chance of losing your shirt. Yes, you'll have a tax shelter, but will you have a retirement shelter? Whether you want to invest in this variation of the IRA and Keogh accounts depends on your emotional makeup. If you're inclined to take chances, go ahead; if you're not, stay away from them. Just one final word: If you're a dyed-in-the-wool gambler, you can direct the bank or investment house handling your account to put your money into the kind of investments *you* choose. These kinds of IRA and Keogh accounts are called "self-directed." Unless you know what you're doing, stay away from them.

To sum up concerning IRA and Keogh accounts: They save you tax dollars now and after retirement. That can be regarded as extra interest on your accounts. With current IRA and Keogh accounts, your interest is below the rate of inflation. However, your tax savings can be regarded as interest as well. What those savings amount to depends on your tax bracket, and to figure out just how to convert tax savings into percent interest requires a bit of mathematics. If you have an accountant, you can ask him to figure it out for you; if not, ask the bank officer where you're thinking of setting up one or other of the accounts. Should the total interest beat the rate of inflation, then consider a bank IRA or Keogh. If not, consider any other version that does.

54. GOLD.

"Dr. Meltzer, I've read book after book after book on gold, and I still can't understand why it goes up when the rate of inflation goes up. Can you help me?" That's a question I keep hearing that doesn't surprise me in the least, because most economists don't talk the language of the person in the street. To understand how gold is priced all you need do is apply some common sense, as follows.

Consider all the money in this country as being a big pie. Let's say the pie is worth $100 billion. Now let's say there's 100 billion ounces of gold available to buy that pie. So, divide 100 billion dollars by 100 billion ounces of gold, and you get the value of an ounce of gold—$1. But you remember, inflation is caused in part by deficit spending, the government pouring more money into the pie. Let's say the government puts another $100 billion into the pie, bringing the total to $200 billion. Do that division again, and you'll see the price of gold has shot up to $2. As the government pours more money into the pie—as inflation increases—the price of gold goes up and up. It's that simple.

In practice gold goes up and down from day to day, but the long-range trend is determined by the rate of inflation. "But," you might ask, "if I held gold, I would just stay neck and neck with inflation. I want to make profits. Why do you say gold is a good investment?" Let me answer that question part by part, as follows:

About staying neck and neck with inflation: The people who establish the price of gold each day on the London Exchange anticipate that inflation is going to rise consistently, so the price is pegged to take future inflation into account. In other words, if price A would just give the investor a break-even return on his money in terms of inflation, the Londoners fix the price of gold at A+ so the return is certain to beat the rate of inflation. And about is it a good investment: I didn't say that. Remember, good or bad depends on your life situation. How would you as an individual react to the conditions of buying and selling gold? Let's get into that now.

• *Buying gold.* There are several ways.

You can buy gold coins. All you have to do to find dealers is look in your Yellow Pages. But don't buy *any* gold coin on sale. You want liquidity, the ability to find a buyer when you need to sell—and to find the buyer quickly. There are three kinds on the market at the time this book went to press that provide you with that liquidity. They are Mexico's 50-peso Centenario, the Austrian 100-crown piece, and the South African Kruggerand. How liquid are they? Well, the Centenario has been around for sixty or so years, and more than 17 million of them have passed hands. There's no trouble buying any of these three standard gold coins, and there's no trouble selling them.

I should make a little digression here about the people who think the sky will fall. They say, hoard gold—because even when civilization fails, gold will be valuable. I don't dispute that. If you think that civilization is going to fail, if you think that this mighty nation is going to go on the rocks, then it will be mighty comforting to you to know that you have a store of gold. But I don't feel that way about the future of America. I know—I repeat, I *know*—America will grow stronger and more powerful every year at home and abroad. I wouldn't buy gold because our skies are going to fall. I don't own any gold, because I think there's a much, much better way to hedge against inflation—and that's owning my own home. I made that decision according to *my* life situation. You'll make yours according to *your* situation. But to do so you must have the facts; so let's get back to talking about buying and selling gold.

To make a significant investment, you have to put up a lot of cash—at the time this book was written, from $400 to over $500 per coin for any of the three coins I've already mentioned. There's another coin that is becoming increasingly popular, the Canadian Maple Leaf, and that sold for a little over $400. The coins contain 1 troy ounce of pure gold, except the 50-peso piece, which contains 1.2 troy ounces (and is, therefore, the most expensive), and the 100-crown piece, which contains .9832 of an ounce (and is, therefore, the least expensive). So if you're buying ten coins, you're in for $4,000 to $5,000 plus the dealer's commission. You have to put it up in cash. There's no dealer who will sell you gold coins on credit.

The next question that comes up is: "Should you borrow to buy gold coins?" That's once again up to you. You don't earn interest on gold; you can't see your growth in a bank statement every month. It may take a year before the value of the coins gives you a return higher than the inflation rate. How do you feel about paying back your debt month after month, while you see no physical return for your investment? If that makes you feel uncomfortable, don't borrow. But if you can take personal deficit financing with a smile, consider it. Once again, if you can borrow for a little and get a lot, it's a sensible thing to do.

You can buy gold bullion. That's pure gold. You can buy it in bars, or lumps, or even in gold dust. A kilobar, which is a bar of gold bullion weighing 35 ounces, is the minimum some dealers will sell you. Hold your hat—that costs, at the time this book goes to press, about $20,000. Have you got that kind of money to invest? If you have, are you willing to put all of it into gold? On the other hand, there are some dealers who are willing to sell you a few ounces. Look for the names of the dealers in the Yellow Pages, and if gold is something you're interested in, call up and ask, "What's the minimum quantity I can buy?" Be prepared when you buy, and again when you sell, to pay commissions; also be prepared to take at least 2 percent less than the market price when you sell. Both costs cut down on your profits. But still, if gold prices go up, say, 20 percent a year, and your costs are 4 percent a year —commissions, and discount on market price—you're getting 16 percent return on your money, and that beats inflation. If you can borrow for 5 percent, that gives you an 11 percent profit, and you can stay ahead of inflation—but not by much. If you think that gold will go up by 25 percent, you can borrow at a higher rate. But with gold bullion, as with gold coins, you know the rate of gain will be higher than the rate of inflation, but you don't know by how much. If there's a threat of war, it could go sky-high. If there's a threat of the possibility of our country licking inflation, it could sink so low it might take years to recover. In buying gold of any kind, there's a big risk factor, which is multiplied when you buy the gold with borrowed money. Are you that kind of a heavy risk-taker?

You can buy gold futures. Talking about risks, this is pure gambling. Now for one of my digressions: I hate gambling. No gambler dies rich. I've never seen a happy gambler. I think it's an abuse of money of the worst kind. That's why you'll see nothing about the stock market in these pages. Playing the stock market is as much gambling as playing the games in Las Vegas or Atlantic City. And if there's anything worse than that as far as gambling goes, it's playing the commodities market, which to my mind is the worst form of gambling. And that's what you're playing, the commodities market, when you buy gold futures.

Let me tell you about the commodities market. What are commodities? Hogs are commodities, cattle are commodities, grains are commodities—there are about forty different kinds of commodities of that nature which are traded on the commodity markets. You trade through your commodity broker (you can find commodity brokers listed in the Yellow Pages). You do it by borrowing directly from the broker. That is to say, you buy on margin, which as I told you before, means you buy on credit. All you do is put up 5 to 25 percent of the purchase price—which means your margin is 5 to 25 percent. What you're buying is a contract in a commodity to be delivered at a *future* date. You never see the commodity—what would you do with hogs? You never even see the contract. All you know is that you've given an order to buy.

Now, gold is a commodity. Let's see what happens when you buy a contract for a future delivery of gold. You call up your broker and ask what the price of gold is pegged at for six months from now; let's call that date December 24. Your broker tells you it's $500 per ounce. You say, "Buy me a contract for 100 ounces deliverable on December 24." That's $50,000 worth of gold you're buying. The broker says, "Okay. Send me your check for $10,000." That's your investment; you're buying the gold future on 20 percent margin. What you're doing is gambling that on December 24 the price of gold will not be $500 per ounce, but something more than $500.

Let's say your hunch is right. December 24 rolls around and the price of gold is $520 an ounce. Your contract is now worth $52,000. You sell it, and make a profit of $2,000 (less broker's fees) on an investment of $10,000. That's about a 20 percent return on your money in six months; and in terms of annual return that's 40 percent! What a Christmas present!

But suppose your hunch was wrong. Let's say that on December 24, the price of gold is only $480. You'll have to sell the contract for $48,000 and take a $2,000 loss (plus broker's fees). That's a 20 percent loss on your $10,000 over six months; 40 percent over a year. And if during the six months before delivery date the value of gold should fall, your broker will call you up and ask for more margin. Are you willing to risk taking a big loss? Are you the kind of person who can pour more money into your investment when its value is going down? Very few of us are. Investing in gold futures, or in the commodity market in general, is only for the gamblers among us.

You can buy stocks in gold mining companies. This would seem to be on the surface a sound investment. There are two reasons for that. One, when the price of gold goes up—and it will probably continue to go up—the value of the stocks will go up. In recent years, while other blue-chip stocks barely kept up with inflation, gold stock values increased at about twice the rate of inflation. But any stock, as I said before, is a gamble. Do you know how much gold there is in the mine? It could be depleted before you know, and the value of the stock could go crashing down. Do you know how well the mining company is being managed? Of course not. And a badly managed company sooner or later will show deficits, and its stock will go downhill. One other thing: Stocks go up and down for no reason at all sometimes, and you could be caught in a down market. On the positive side, I'll say this: If you must dabble in the stock market, gold mining company stocks are your best buy. You can buy them on margin from your broker, and if they can continue to rise, your investments can bring you in a return well above the rate of inflation. But remember, it's for risk-takers only.

You can minimize the risk by buying through a mutual fund. You have the safety of owning a share in a pie made up of the stocks of many different gold mining companies. Some of these funds are no-load, which means you don't have to pay broker's fees, and—best of all—you can buy in for as little as $500. Some of these mutual funds offer another attraction. It's this: When gold is going down, you can call up and switch your money to another fund managed by the same investment firm. Returns on these kinds of mutual funds run well above the rate of inflation, and should appeal to the investor who wants to limit risk and still take advantage of the returns that come with taking risks.

55. INVESTMENT NO-NO'S.

• *Valuables.* The next question I'm asked when I've finished discussing gold is usually "What about *silver?*" or "What about *diamonds?*" or "What about other *precious stones?*" And I answer very simply, "At the moment, they simply don't beat the rate of inflation, and I think it's a waste of time to discuss any kind of investment that doesn't." The same applies to valuable *collectibles*—things which, as the name suggests, people collect, such as art works, rare books, autographs, vintage wines, and rare coins. I want to make one thing clear. It is possible that you can buy a collectible and in a few years make a fortune by reselling it, and you hear stories like that all the time. But you also hear stories about people who win millions in a lottery. I think you get my point.

• *Foreign currency.* And while I'm on the subject of investment no-no's, let me say I'm against investing in the currency of other nations, particularly *Swiss francs.* You don't make your money from interest in Swiss banks, because they pay very little, 3 to 4 percent. What you make your money from is the decreasing value of the American dollar. As the dollar declines, your Swiss franc comes to be worth more and more; so over the last decade, the actual interest on Swiss francs averaged about 10 percent. That keeps up with inflation, but it doesn't beat it. I predict that the dollar will go stronger in the years to come, so you won't even earn that 10 percent. Besides, I don't think it's patriotic to put your money to work in another country. If our country is to grow stronger, your investments should be made here.

• *Bonds.*   A bond is another form of IOU, issued by corporations and government agencies. As a voter you know there's always a "bond issue" to be voted on—which means the government wants your permission to borrow money for new bridges, or new jail houses, or new highways, or something or other. The drawbacks of bonds are threefold. One, they don't as a rule bring in interest higher than the rate of inflation. Two, they're usually long-term obligations, averaging about thirty years, which means that you're going to get back the money you put into them in the form of very, very shrunken dollars. And three, there's a financial rule of thumb which says: As interest rates go up, the values of bonds go down—and interest rates are climbing steadily. That means if you want to sell your bonds before maturity date, some decades in the future, you'll get much, much less for your bonds than what you paid for them.

There's one kind of bond that can beat inflation, but only if your income is in the top brackets. I'm talking about *tax-free bonds.* Since a great many of these tax-free bonds are issued by cities all over the nation, you're probably familiar with them as "tax-free municipals." When you buy a tax-free bond, you don't have to pay the IRS tax on your interest (dividends). That's the same as increasing your interest. But if you sit down with a computer, you'll find that you'll have to be in at least the 50 percent tax bracket before the interest on most bonds creeps above the rate of inflation. But even if you're in the higher tax brackets, bonds are a questionable investment for the other reasons I've mentioned. Besides, if you're looking for tax-free income, you can just take out an All Saver. Remember, an individual can get $1,000 interest tax-free from October 1, 1981, to December 31, 1982 on All Savers, and a couple can get $2,000 interest tax-free.

While I'm against bonds as an investment, in all fairness I'd like to tell you about the new *floating-rate tax-free bond funds.* These are mutual funds, and what you buy are shares in high-rated state, municipal and corporate bonds—the interest on which is tax-free. What sets these new bond funds apart is that the interest rate is adjusted weekly to current interest rates. That means the value of your bonds remains about the same as when you bought them. You can't lose, and you can redeem your investment at any time. To get more information, see under Bonds, under *Sources for More Information* at the end of this book.

• *Real estate.*   One more type of investment I put on my no-no list is *speculating in real estate*. That needs explanation because everybody who knows me is aware that I believe land and housing are the bedrock investments of our times. But if there's one business in the world that requires long, long experience to succeed in, that's real estate speculating. Yes, you *can* buy raw land for almost nothing—there's some land you can even get free from the government—and develop it, and make a killing. But do *you* know how to buy raw land? Do *you* know how to develop it? When you buy plots of land from developers, you can get stung pretty badly. And yes, you can buy rundown property with government grants, and restore it to give it a big price tag. But do *you* know what property to buy? Do *you* know how to restore property?

There are lots of books around about how to make a million in real estate with nothing down; but let me tell you, I know this field inside and out, and there's no way of doing that without years and years of experience and know-how, and even then it takes nerves of steel and a risk-taking personality of the first order to pull it off. There's just too much involved in real estate speculation for the average person to get involved. REITs—real estate investment trusts, a kind of mutual fund for real estate investments—seemed at one time to be the answer to the small investor's desire to participate in the huge profits of real estate. But even though these funds were managed by real estate experts who allegedly knew everything there was to know about purchasing office buildings, shopping malls, large apartment complexes, and so on, they crashed in 1974. They're still around, but they're risk investments.

• *Second-deed trusts.*   "Are they risky, too?" I'm often asked. When this question is addressed to me at a seminar, I turn to the audience and ask, "How many of you know what a second-deed trust is? Raise your hands." Not many hands are raised. So I explain briefly. "Suppose you're buying a house, and you can only raise X dollars toward the down payment. It's not enough; you still need Y dollars. The real estate agent brings in a third party who says, 'Okay, you need $4,000. Give me a second deed trust for $5,000, which you can pay back in three years.' During the three years the investor collects monthly interest at the current rates plus principal. At the end of the three years, he's gotten back $5,000 for his $4,000 plus interest on the $5,000. That's a return of far better than 20 percent on his money."

At this point the audience oohs and aahhs. "But," I ask them, "do you think somebody who can't raise the down payment for his home is in a good financial position?" "No," they answer. "And," I go on, "would you like to invest your hard-earned money with somebody who's not in a good financial position?" "No!" they shout. "So think twice," I advise them, "before some real estate broker talks you into buying a second deed trust."

And I want to conclude my list of no-no's by stating again that any investment in the stock market is pure gambling.

BERNARD MELTZER'S ADVICE ON THE BEST INVESTMENTS TO BEAT INFLATION

This advice box will be longer than the others, because I want to repeat what I said earlier in the book. I'm not advising money sophisticates and gamblers. I'm talking to everyday Americans who want to see their money grow faster than the rate of inflation, and who want to see it grow safely. Certainly, if you've come this far in this book, you're one of those people. Here, then, are my recommendations for you:

Short- and long-term CDs, certain money funds, variable premium deferred annuities, IRA and Keogh accounts linked to inflation-beating instruments, All Savers, gold coin or bullion—and the best investment of all, your home.

You can buy all of these investments by borrowing. Just remember my advice on how to get a mortgage and how to borrow for investment purposes.

Now let's see how your life situation determines which investments are right for you.

Chapter 13

Investing According to
Your Life Situation

There are so many variables in dealing with investing according to your life situation that the only way I could give you specific advice is if we sat down together and had a talk, or if you called me on one of my broadcasts. As I implied in my opening remarks, I hope we can meet one way or another, and I hope one day I can be of voice-to-voice help to you as I have been to so many others. In the meantime, what I'm going to do here is give you general advice, which I think you'll be able to fit to your particular case.

Let me begin by drawing a very rapid overall picture of your life situation from three angles—your income, your age, and your personality. So far as your income is concerned, I'm assuming you're an average American. If you weren't you wouldn't be reading this book. So far as age is concerned, I'm going to divide people into three groups: from age twenty-one to thirty-four, from age thirty-five to age sixty-four, and from age sixty-five to—well, I hope you live to be more than a hundred. And so far as personality is concerned, you're either a member of the no-risk group or the risk group; you either tend to take risks as a matter of course or you don't.

When I make this point about risk and no-risk personalities, there's always somebody who pops up and says, "Dr. Meltzer, I don't know what kind of personality I am. Can you help me?" I say, "Of course," and I ask the following questions.

56. HOW TO DISCOVER YOUR INVESTMENT PERSONALITY.

	YES	NO
Are you frequently guilty of speeding?	☐	☐
Do you prefer short-term gains to long-term gains?	☐	☐
Do you like making your own decisions, in particular investment decisions?	☐	☐
Would you rather be self-employed than work for a steady salary?	☐	☐
Do you feel pleasantly excited when you're in any risk situation?	☐	☐
Do you like to have your own way, even when others tell you your way is wrong?	☐	☐
Do you feel that success in life is a matter of being at the right place at the right time?	☐	☐
In a crisis situation, are you cool and collected?	☐	☐
Do you enjoy playing cards, or spending time at the race track or a casino?	☐	☐
Can you take a defeat, then start all over again determined to win?	☐	☐

I would say if you answered five or more of those questions yes, you have a risk personality.

57. THE RIGHT INVESTMENTS FOR YOU AT ANY AGE.

In the advice that follows I'm assuming that your life cycle—the way your income changes with the years, and the way you pass from one stage of family life to another—is the same as the average American's.

• *The right investments for you at age 21 to 34.* These are the years when you're getting set in life and building a family. You have large basic everyday expenses. You need, and you buy, adequate protection for yourself and your family—life insurance, health insurance, an education fund. You may have more than one car. There's little money you can use at your own discretion.

If you're a no-risk personality, invest in your home and in your security umbrella. I've already told you how. If you have some discretionary money left over, invest in a Keogh or IRA that will provide interest higher than the rate of inflation. *Don't* borrow to invest at this stage of your life.

If you're a risk personality, invest in your home and in your security umbrella. These are the foundation investments no matter which kind of personality you are. But as a risk personality, build your savings umbrella to cover a twelve-month period, not just a six-month period. The chances are you'll be changing jobs more frequently, and some of them won't work out, so there will be more frequent periods of unemployment than if you were a no-risk personality. If you do have some discretionary income, put aside 80 percent of it for a Keogh or IRA that will provide interest higher than the rate of inflation. Then get your feet wet in risk investments with money funds, where you can't be hurt too badly. *Don't* borrow to invest at this stage of your life.

• *The right investments for you at age 35 to 64.*   During this period, you're in a pattern of steady growth—your children are growing up, you're growing as a human being, your income is growing. Toward the last years of this period, your expenses dwindle as your children fly from the nest. You now have more money to invest than before.

If you're a no-risk personality, stay with your Keogh or IRA, then divide the rest of your discretionary money as follows: 50 percent in easy-access CDs, 40 percent in a variable annuity, and 10 percent in gold coins or bullion. You're well established in life now, so to make your money grow even faster, borrow money with which to invest.

If you're a risk personality, stay with your Keogh or IRA, and bolster your chances of a happy retirement by putting 50 percent of your discretionary money in a variable annuity. Put another 25 percent in mutual funds; they have an element of risk that should please you. Split the remaining 25 percent between gold futures; and, since you're a human being and you'll try whether I advise you against it or not, the stock market. But learn something about the stock market before you take the plunge. Look under *Sources for More Information* at the end of this book for data on Stocks and Securities.

• *The right investments for you at age 65 to 100+.*   If you prepared for retirement from the time you started work, as I strongly advise, then in and around the years you retire, you have a bonanza waiting for you. There will be hundreds of thousands of dollars—perhaps more than a million—from your IRA or Keogh, and large sums of the same order from your variable annuity; and you can sell your house at an enormous profit. You can also convert your life insurance policy from whole life to term, and collect another big wad of money. And since in all likelihood you'll be in a much lower tax bracket when you retire, anything that can be taxed will be taxed at a lower rate. At the same time, you have virtually no responsibilities toward your children financially, you're no longer tied down to them physically, and your nine-to-five days are over forever. You're rich and you're free. You can do whatever you like with your money. The world's your oyster. What a wonderful feeling!

But you must look to the future. You have many, many years of life ahead of you. Whether you're a no-risk personality or a risk personality, you have to invest your money in such a way that it will supplement your income to provide enough money monthly to keep you and your spouse in the life-style to which you have become accustomed. Your remaining funds should be invested in any way that makes you happy. It's your life, and retirement years could be the best part of it. Enjoy!

But if you haven't prepared for retirement—as is the case with too many people—the choice is limited to investment in safe funds which will bring you a return higher than the rate of inflation. Whether you're a no-risk or a risk personality, that's the only way you can go when you feel the financial pinch of the retirement years. If you decide to sell your house and live in a rented apartment, you'll have a very large nest egg to invest, and that could relieve the financial strain. Under no circumstance take risks with that nest egg, even if you're a risk personality. You need income, so invest it in safe easy-access CDs. That's all. Quite a contrast between being prepared for retirement and not being prepared!

The *New York Daily News* said about me, "Bernard Meltzer is a rock of common sense in a world gone mad." I don't think the world has gone mad; I have too much faith in humanity to think that. But I do think that many, many so-called experts have lost touch with common sense. I hope you feel that my common-sense advice has been useful to you. I feel it a great honor that you've read my book, and I look forward to hearing from you soon.

So long. This is your friend Bernard Meltzer, saying goodbye, and God bless you all.

Sources for
More Information

Almost all these sources are free, but there are a few that charge a minimal fee, and I've indicated them. Some of the sources are commercial; I'm recommending them only as places to go to get information. It's up to you to decide if you want to use their services. The sources are listed alphabetically by subject matter.

ANNUITIES

Spectrum
Massachusetts Financial Service of Boston
200 Berkley St.
Boston, MA 02111

Seel and Seel Financial Planners
51 Picardy Court
Walnut Creek, CA 94596

BONDS, FLOATING RATE TAX-FREE FUNDS

E. F. Hutton
One Battery Park Plaza
New York, NY 10004

Shearson/American Express, Inc.
Unit Trust Dept.
14 Wall St.
New York, NY 10005

BORROWING

National Consumer Finance Association
Washington, DC 20036
1000 16th St., NW

National Foundation for Consumer Credit
1819 H St., NW
Washington, DC 20006

Family Service Association of America
44 E. 23rd St.
New York, NY 10010

CARS

Car Buying Made Easier
Ford Motor Company
The American Road
Dearborn, MI 48121

How to Buy a Used Car
Consumers Union of U.S., Inc.
256 Washington St.
Mt. Vernon, NY 10550
   Write for cost information

Consumer Reports, April and December
Consumers Union of U.S., Inc.
256 Washington St.
Mt. Vernon, NY 10550
   Write for cost information

CREDIT CARDS

National Bank of North America
Visa Card
P.O. Box 469
Huntington Station, NY 11746

CREDIT RATING

Associated Credit Bureaus, Inc.
6767 Southwest Freeway
Houston, TX 77306

CREDIT UNIONS

CUNA
P.O. Box 431
Madison, WI 53701

GOLD

Merrill Lynch, Inc.
P.O. Box 399, Bowling Green Station
New York, NY 10274

Citibank Gold Center
399 Park Ave.
New York, NY 10043

Peak & Co.
1800 K St., NW
Washington, DC 20026

Golconda Investors, Ltd.
P.O. Box 126
Glenford, NY 12433

GOLD COINS

Auric United Corporation
15746 Interstate Highway
P.O. Box 29568
San Antonio, TX 78229

Numisco
1423 West Fullerton Ave.
Chicago, IL 60614

Deak-Perera Co.
630 Fifth Ave.
New York, NY 10020

HOUSING

Basic Housing Inspection
HEW
Room 1587, Parklane Building
5600 Fisher's Lane
Rockwell, MD 20852

Questions About Condominiums
HUD
Washington, DC 20410

Condominium Buyer's Guide
NAHB
15th and M Sts., NW

Washington, DC 20005
  Fee $1

Mobile Home Manufacturers Association
Box 35
Chantilly, VA 22021

DSI List of Satisfactory Contractors
HUD Printing Office
451 7th St., SW
Washington, DC 20410

INSURANCE, ALL TYPES

Consumer News, Inc.
813 National Press Building
Washington, DC 20045

INSURANCE, AUTOMOBILE AND LIABILITY

Insurance Information Institute
110 Williams St.
New York, NY 10038

KEOGH AND IRA

Plymouth-Home National Bank
34 School St.
Brockton, MA 02403

Lincoln Trust Co.
P.O. Box 5831
Denver, CO 80297

Farmer's Bank of Delaware
Box 8853
Wilmington, DE 19899

MONEY FUNDS

The Value Line Cash Fund, Inc.
711 Third Ave.
New York, NY 10017

The Dreyfus Group
767 Fifth Ave.
New York, NY 10022

Franklin Money Fund
155 Bovet Road
San Mateo, CA 94402

MORTGAGES

Federal Housing Administration
Department of Housing and Urban Development
451 7th St., SW
Washington, DC 20410

Veterans Administration
810 Vermont Ave.
Washington, DC 20420

Farm Credit Administration
490 L'Enfant Plaza East, SW
Washington, DC 20578

MUTUAL FUNDS

Directory
No-Load Mutual Fund Association
Valley Forge, PA 19481

No-Load Mutual Funds Membership List
Investment Company Institute
1775 K St., NW
Washington, DC 20006

20th Century Investors
605 W. 47th St.
Kansas City, MO 64112

The Rowe Price Group
100 E. Pratt St.
Baltimore, MD 21202

SAVINGS

National Bank Examiner
Comptroller of the Treasury
Washington, DC 20219

United States League of Savings Associations
111 E. Wacker Drive
Chicago, IL 60601

United Dime Bank
1065 Avenue of the Americas
New York, NY 10020

STOCKS AND SECURITIES

Securities and Exchange Commission
500 North Capital St., NW
Washington, DC 20549

New Investor Package
Public Information Office
New York Stock Exchange
11 Wall St.
New York, NY 10005

Charles Schwab & Company
1 2nd St.
San Francisco, CA 94105

Quick & Reilly, Inc.
120 Wall St.
New York, NY 10005

National Association of Investment Clubs
1515 E. Eleven Mile Road
Royal Oak, MI 48067

The Handbook of Securities of the U.S. Government
First Boston Corp.
20 Exchange Place
New York, NY 10005
  Fee $10

WARRANTIES

Federal Trade Commission
Division of Special Statutes
Washington, DC 20580